By Henry Pleasants

VIENNA'S GOLDEN YEARS OF MUSIC
selected, translated and edited
from the collected works of Eduard Hanslick (1950)

THE AGONY OF MODERN MUSIC (*1955*)

THE MUSICAL JOURNEYS OF LOUIS SPOHR
selected, translated and edited
from Louis Spohr's Selbstbiographie (*1961*)

DEATH OF A MUSIC?
The Decline of the European Tradition
and the Rise of Jazz (*1961*)

THE MUSICAL WORLD OF ROBERT SCHUMANN
selected, translated and edited
from the critical writings of Robert Schumann (1965)

THE GREAT SINGERS
From the Dawn of Opera to Our Own Time (*1967*)

Serious Music— and All That Jazz!

AN ADVENTURE IN MUSIC CRITICISM

BY

Henry Pleasants

SIMON AND SCHUSTER · NEW YORK

FIRST UNITED STATES PRINTING

SBN 671-20185-9
LIBRARY OF CONGRESS CATALOG CARD NUMBER: 69-12093
DESIGNED BY EDITH FOWLER
MANUFACTURED IN THE UNITED STATES OF AMERICA
BY AMERICAN BOOK—STRATFORD PRESS, INC.

To the memory of Constant Lambert (1905–1951), who, in Music Ho!: A Study of Music in Decline *(1934), was twenty years ahead of any of us in discerning the new crosscurrents in the evolution of Western music in the twentieth century*

ACKNOWLEDGMENTS

THIS BOOK deals with many areas of contemporary music, in none of which am I either a specialist or an expert. I count myself fortunate, however, in numbering specialists and experts in each of them among my friends and in being able to call upon them for comment, correction, criticism and suggestion. I wish here to express my thanks to those who read the whole typescript in various stages of preparation or those parts of it dealing with their own particular fields of professional activity, noting at the same time that the inclusion of their names should not be construed as evidence of their agreement with all that the book sets forth: Howard Boatwright, John Dankworth, Jack Elliott, Hugo Friedhofer, Friedrich Gulda, Quincy Jones, Charles Keil, H. C. Robbins Landon, Gene Lees, Erich Leinsdorf, George London, Gerry Mulligan, Dr. William B. Ober, Robert Share, Robert Shelton, Adrian Sunshine and Phil Woods.

I am particularly indebted to Gene Lees, upon whose articles on music in the motion pictures in *HiFi/Stereo Review* and *High Fidelity* I have drawn for my chapter on The Lyric Theater.

A special word of thanks to Billy Taylor, from whose playing and conversation during many fondly remembered evenings at the Hickory House in New York I learned more about jazz and the enjoyment of jazz than from any other single source.

And to Henry Simon, as so often in the past, the most helpful of editors, and his associates at Simon and Schuster, Mrs. Edith Fowler, Mrs. Evelyn Gendel, Mrs. Ann Maulsby and Mrs. Sophie Sorkin.

Contents

Music, architecture and painting, as well as poetry and oratory, are to deduce their laws and rules from the general sense and taste of mankind, and not from the principles of those arts themselves; or in other words, the taste is not to conform to the art, but the art to the taste.

—JOSEPH ADDISON in *The Spectator*, April 3, 1711

Bars 1, 3, 5, 7 and 9 begin on a B (natural or flat) or a G, and eventually rise, usually via a B to a C natural or D flat. Bars 2, 4, 6, 8 and 10 begin on a C sharp or an A (natural or flat, enharmonically expressed as G sharp in bar 10), and all except bar 10 fall through an A. The intervals in this basic pattern are varieties of second or third, and the first real evidence of interpenetration is when the perfect fourth which begins bar 3 is echoed at the end of bar 4. The enharmonic equivalent of these same notes (A flat/E flat: G sharp/D sharp) will be stated in bar 11 as evidence of complete interpenetration of one 'side' by the other. In bar 5 the interval of a semitone appears for the first time in an odd-numbered bar. In bar 8 an even-numbered bar has the crucial B flat, which so far has been peculiar to the odds. . . .

—ARNOLD WHITTALL in a discussion of Webern's
Opus 16 in *The Musical Times* (London), April 1967

Delight must be the basis and aim of this art. Simple melody—clear rhythm!

—ROSSINI in a letter of June 21, 1868

Music is a science that would have us laugh and sing and dance.

GUILLAUME MACHAUT (c.1300–1377)

Introduction

In *The Agony of Modern Music* I advanced the proposition that neither Schoenberg's twelve-tone system nor the neo-classical movement, led initially by Stravinsky, had offered a satisfactory exit from the technical cul-de-sac recognized by Serious composers everywhere during the first two decades of this century. And I suggested that a more truly modern idiom was to be found in jazz.

I carried this idea farther in a second book, published in England, *Death of a Music?*, with the subtitle, *The Decline of the European Tradition and the Rise of Jazz*. Since the publication of these two books, in 1955 and 1961 respectively, jazz, as a popular style, has been largely superseded for the younger generations throughout the world by a variety of related styles imprecisely identified as "rock" and "pop."

The present book is an attempt to place a succession of Afro-American styles—ragtime, jazz, swing, bop, rhythm-and-blues, country-and-western, rock and pop—in perspective as an idiomatic phenomenon within the centuries-long span of the evolution of Western music.

And since my conclusions will be regarded as radically

unorthodox by most music lovers of all categories, it seems appropriate to begin autobiographically. With a book in which contemporary Serious and contemporary Popular music will constantly be juxtaposed, it seems to me essential that the reader know something of the author's own musical background, upbringing, schooling, practice and taste. The reader should know, above all, whether the author speaks from the point of view and experience of the Serious or the Popular musician. I dislike the terms *serious* (or *classical*) and *popular,* and I shall have much to say about them and against them; but they are part of our accepted musical terminology, and I shall be using them conventionally even while attempting to demonstrate the misleading and prejudicial implications of their conventional use, registering my dissent by recourse to the upper case.

I come from the world of Serious music. I studied voice, piano, *solfège* and theory, first at the Philadelphia Musical Academy and the Curtis Institute of Music, later privately with a number of teachers in the United States and Europe. From 1930 to 1942 I was music critic of the *Philadelphia Evening Bulletin* and from 1945 to 1955 central European musical correspondent of *The New York Times.* Most of my books and magazine articles have been about Serious music, including my translations of Eduard Hanslick, Louis Spohr and Robert Schumann and, more recently, an original work, *The Great Singers* (1967).

As a young critic I was concerned primarily with modern music. In Philadelphia, in the 1930s, my curiosity was stimulated, if rarely satisfied, by the adventurous programs of Leopold Stokowski and the Philadelphia Orchestra. When still only twenty-one, I covered the first American performances of *Wozzeck* in Philadelphia and New York, a joint production of the Philadelphia Orchestra and the Philadelphia Grand Opera Company under Stokowski's direction. ("Already the field is divided," I wrote, "between those who find in it no satisfactory musical form and those for whom it represents an idealization of the Wagnerian principles of music drama. Probably it will continue to have its adherents and its opponents, for it is made of enduring qualities. Behind it lies a background of learning, sincerity, technical accomplishment and, perhaps, genius.")

I heard and reviewed all the new music current in that decade, including Stokowski's spectacular productions of Schoenberg's *Gurrelieder*, Stravinsky's *Le Sacre du Printemps* and *Oedipus Rex*, Carlos Chávez's ballet *HP* and Prokofiev's *Le Pas d'Acier*. In the opera house were the Metropolitan Opera Association's Philadelphia premières of Louis Gruenberg's *Emperor Jones*, Howard Hanson's *Merry Mount* and Deems Taylor's *The King's Henchman* and *Peter Ibbetson*. Among hundreds of instrumental works were excerpts from Alban Berg's *Lulu*, Anton Webern's Symphony for Small Orchestra, and the violin concertos of Schoenberg and Berg. I was, for most of that time, the Philadelphia correspondent of the League of Composers' periodical, *Modern Music*, and with Tibor Serly I contributed to *Modern Music* one of the first extensive articles to appear in the United States on Béla Bartók.

In central Europe, after the war, I observed the sudden propagation of serial music, sponsored primarily by the German and Austrian radio institutions and music publishers. I attended and reviewed the festivals at Donaueschingen (Pierre Boulez, John Cage, Luigi Dallapiccola, Luigi Nono, etc.), the Musica Viva concerts in Munich, the modern music programs of the Konzerthaus in Vienna, and so on. In the opera house I heard and covered the premières of Gottfried von Einem's *Dantons Tod* and *Der Prozess*, Carl Orff's *An-*

tigone, Benjamin Britten's *The Rape of Lucretia,* Rolf Liebermann's *Penelope,* Werner Egk's *Die Irische Legende,* Boris Blacher's *Abstrakte Oper No. 1* and Ernst Křenek's *Pallas Athene Weint.*

It was during this postwar period that I began to have misgivings about the validity of the new music, and of the new serial music particularly. It gave me no pleasure, no sense of any salutary esthetic reward. Nor did it seem to give pleasure to anyone else. Indeed, there seemed to be no pleasurable objective. Composers were concerned with progress, or at least with sustaining a façade of modernity. This produced, curiously, a stifling uniformity. What was trumpeted as progress was, it seemed to me, an exclusive fashion, its immunity from plebeian emulation guaranteed by adherence to the dogma that pleasure, which all the great music of the past had given, was no longer admirable or even pertinent.

What makes a music contemporary, in my view, is not originality, or novelty, or theoretical conclusions, or the mere circumstance of contemporary authorship. It is acceptance by a considerable audience, documenting the musician's communicative success and his mastery of a musical vernacular. Viability is the primary criterion, establishing the disciplines that may then govern the artist's pursuit of excellence.

The Serious composer, good or bad, was not finding acceptance *even with his own Serious music public;* and this was a public predisposed in his favor as no previous public had ever been. Certainly he was finding acceptance with no other. And so I asked myself: What contemporary music does address itself successfully to a large audience in a language the audience understands? The answer, at the time, was jazz.

I had had little experience with jazz, and knew next to nothing about it. While in secondary school I had sung briefly with a dance band. As a young critic in Philadelphia I had reviewed Paul Whiteman at the Academy of Music and the Benny Goodman band at Robin Hood Dell. I had been exposed to Tommy Dorsey's band while reviewing a motion picture at the Earle Theater. I had heard George Gershwin, and I was aware of a way of singing called crooning. What I had heard I had liked, but I hadn't paid much attention to it. My heart and mind belonged to the symphony orchestra, the opera house and the recital hall.

I assumed then, as most people do now, that there was "good" music and Popular music, and I was identified happily with "good" music. Nothing in the attitudes of those around me, including those who found their pleasure in Popular music, was calculated to disturb my complacency. Not even the lovers of Popular music, or the early jazz fans, questioned the superiority of "good" music, or my own superior status as a Serious music critic.

Had my complacency been less secure, it would have been shaken by a single experience that remains among the most vivid and exciting memories of my life in music. It must have been about 1934, in any case shortly after the founding of the American Newspaper Guild. To raise funds for the new organization we gave a ball at the Masonic Temple on North Broad Street. Music for dancing was provided by the then fashionable band of Russ Columbo. But some early jazz enthusiasts among us insisted that there be a "hot" band, too; and so I was introduced to the music of Sidney Bechet.

I have no idea who was playing with him that night. The names meant nothing to me, although there were probably now-sainted ones among them. But Bechet I did not forget. From ten or eleven o'clock until three or four in the morning I never moved from a spot barely ten feet from the stand where he was holding forth. What he whispered and shouted and sang on that curious soprano saxophone of his came right through to me. It was a kind of inspired minstrelsy—joyous, despairing, hopeful, tender, exultant, forceful, compassionate —and always eloquently communicative. Bechet was, above all, a jubilant musician, and never more exuberantly inventive than when he could feel his own fervor in music-making coming back to him from his listeners.

But I drew no conclusions from my own pleasure, and it remained an isolated experience. Now, in the early 1950s, it all came back to me. I was living in Switzerland, and the most popular jazz musician in Switzerland, more traditional in its jazz taste than neighboring Germany or Austria, was—Sidney Bechet. He was based in Paris then, and working with a French group. I took up jazz where I had left it twenty years before, at the feet of Sidney Bechet. And I knew now how to treasure what I heard.

I followed him wherever he went—to Zurich, Bern, Lucerne, Lausanne and Geneva. And through him I became aware of things in jazz that I had never thought of before— instrumental virtuosity, ornamentation and embellishment, melodic variations and deviations, phrasings born of a new concept of pulse, the players' pleasure in antiphonal responses, in supporting and complementary counterpoint. Here was a great soloist and virtuoso working from within and out of something that was essentially a spontaneous chamber music.

Nor did my education come only from the musicians. There were the listeners, too, attentive, enraptured and demonstrative. A brilliant or moving solo (or chorus, in jazz parlance) would be rewarded immediately by a burst of applause—no dutiful waiting until the end of the number. The players, I noted, betrayed no annoyance. Rather the contrary. And I was reminded of a letter Mozart had written to his father after the first performance of his Symphony in D (K. 297) in Paris in 1778:

. . . just in the middle of the first Allegro there was a passage which I felt sure must please. The audience were quite carried away—and there was a tremendous burst of applause. But as I knew when I wrote it, what effect it would surely produce, I had introduced the passage again at the close—when there were shouts of *"Da capo!"* The Andante also found favor, but particularly the last Allegro, because having observed that all last as well as first allegros begin here with all the instruments playing together and generally *unisono,* I began mine with two violins only, piano for the first eight bars—followed instantly by a forte; the audience, as I expected, said "hush" at the soft beginning, and when they heard the forte, began at once to clap their hands. I was so happy that as soon as the symphony was over I went off to the Palais Royal, where I had a large ice, said the rosary as I had vowed to do—and went home. . . .

(The English critic Felix Aprahamian, when André Previn played this symphony with the London Symphony Orchestra in February 1967, recalled this letter in his program notes, adding: "It would appear that, coughing excepted, twentieth century London audiences have greater respect for music than Parisian society had in the eighteenth century." This was an accurate reflection of the twentieth century's approach to music in the concert hall. Mozart, I think, would have been appalled.)

But jazz had come a long way since 1934. While no one questioned Bechet's genius, or his place in jazz history, he was looked upon by many as old-fashioned, as a grand primitive. I had much to learn, and Europe, in the 1950s, was as good a place as any to learn it. Jazz was the music of European as well as of American youth, and the best American jazz musi-

21

cians were flocking to Europe to satisfy the demand. Within a year or two I had heard Louis Armstrong, Count Basie, Duke Ellington, Lionel Hampton, Harry James, the Modern Jazz Quartet, several of Norman Granz's Jazz at the Philharmonic caravans with Oscar Peterson, Ella Fitzgerald, Sarah Vaughan, Bill Harris, Roy Eldridge, Charlie Shavers, Illinois Jacquet, Coleman Hawkins and Dizzy Gillespie. I visited the jazz cellars, listened to the Armed Forces Network, to Willis Conover's Music USA programs on the Voice of America, to Sim Copans' programs on Radio Diffusion, to Joachim E. Berendt's radio programs from Germany and to the many excellent local radio jazz programs in Switzerland, including those by Lance Tschannen. I bought records, subscribed to *Down Beat* and *Metronome* and read everything else I could lay my hands on—Marshall Stearns, Leonard Feather, Barry Ulanov, Ralph J. Gleason, John S. Wilson, Whitney Balliett, Nat Hentoff and George T. Simon.

The problems encountered by a Serious musician of my generation and background in coming to terms with jazz belong to a later chapter. They are considerable; and they have a lot to do with the failure of society as a whole to evaluate justly the artistic stature and the genius of the best jazz musicians. It will suffice for the moment to observe that jazz is many different things to many different individuals, and that the term embraces many kinds and qualities of music.

In the United States, on home leave from foreign service, I traveled some ten thousand miles by automobile, the radio turned on most of the way, and I learned some more about the diversity of American music. Jazz, I discovered, was for the urban connoisseurs. The music of the American heartland was what I had always thought of as hillbilly. I learned to call it country-and-western, and to listen to it with pleasure. My explorations in some of the cities led me to gospel song and to rhythm-and-blues, a secular equivalent of gospel song, whose conjunction with country-and-western would shortly explode into rock 'n' roll.

Not until later did I learn about the Popular singers. I was probably influenced at that time by the jazz musicians' distaste for the Hit Parade; and because some of the best singers were singing the hits—and making the hits—I had to wait before becoming aware of the splendid artistry of Bing Crosby, Frank Sinatra, Ella Fitzgerald, Lena Horne, Peggy Lee, Nat King Cole, Perry Como, Tony Bennett, Andy Williams and many more.

But I am running ahead of myself. I had begun to write *The Agony of Modern Music* in 1951. The stimulus had been my conclusion that new contemporary Serious music would not only *probably* be unsatisfactory, but that it *had* to be. The book was an attempt to establish *why*. I had not begun to listen to jazz when I started it, but by 1954, when it went to press, I had heard enough and studied enough to say confidently and, in the view of many readers impudently, that "jazz is modern music, and nothing else is."

An enormous generalization, of course, its admissibility dependent upon how one defines jazz. I may confess now that in stating it thus dogmatically I was influenced by my delight in what I knew would be regarded as an outrageous formulation. Browsing in Leary's Book Store in Philadelphia, I had happened on an old book of Pennsylvania Dutch recipes. Turning to "Scrapple," for which, as a Philadelphian, I have a special affection, I found, at the end of a catalogue of just about every part of a pig but the meat, the defiant conclusion: "This is scrapple, and nothing else is!"

No ifs, howevers, buts or maybes. But in applying the formula to jazz as modern music I discovered that the opinion was more offensive than the manner of its expression. Even those who agreed, more or less secretly, with my assessment of the state of contemporary Serious music found it horrendous. They might concur with the composer who said, privately, "Pleasants is about seventy-five-percent right, but we don't want *him* telling us." But my suggesting that jazz might be a music worth taking seriously, that it might be better music than what the Serious composer was writing, was treason.

I could see nothing treasonable about it, least of all as an American calling attention to an American contribution to Western music that had already been recognized more generously and more discerningly abroad than at home. Not that my motivation had been chauvinistic. I was speaking simply as a musician and student who had found good music where others of my musical background and upbringing had not looked for it.

I did not think then, and I do not think now, that identification with any particular kind of music implies an obligation of exclusive allegiance. One may acknowledge and accept an allegiance to certain standards of aspiration and attainment. I felt that the best jazz of that period represented very high standards indeed, higher, in some respects, than much that was rated highly in the world of Serious music. And I could not agree that an inherited frame of esthetic reference should forever provide the sole criteria by which music and musicians were to be judged.

Even these criteria, I felt, had been disastrously relaxed in the course of the century. I acknowledged no dishonor to the memory of Bach, Handel, Haydn, Mozart, Beethoven, Schubert, Schumann, Brahms, Verdi and Wagner in my enjoyment of Berlin, Kern, Youmans, Gershwin, Porter, Arlen and Rodgers, nor in my delight in the imaginative and tasteful improvisations of Sidney Bechet, Louis Armstrong, Johnny Hodges, Ben Webster, Lawrence Brown, Oscar Peterson, Art Tatum, Billy Taylor, Coleman Hawkins and Stan Getz. Indeed, I found the disparity between Mozart and jazz far less conspicuous than the disparity between Haydn, Mozart and Beethoven, on the one hand, and Schoenberg, Berg, Webern, Dallapiccola, Křenek, Cage and Karlheinz Stockhausen on the other.

I have always been put off by those critics who can speak of Strauss's *Ariadne auf Naxos* and *Capriccio* as Mozartean, who find Nono and Dallapiccola "lyrical," who can take seriously the pseudo-psychopathic nonsense of *Lulu*. Do they really appreciate Mozart? Have they forgotten that the essence of music is song and dance, and that its noblest objective is the sublimation of the beautiful? And if they recognize and applaud the achievement of this objective in Bach, Haydn, Mozart and Beethoven, why, then, do they not insist, as Hanslick did, that it be acknowledged and honored in contemporary music? Or, more to the point, why do they fail to recognize and acknowledge it in the finest productions of the jazz musician?

Some of them do; but it still makes no difference in their assessment of the relative merits of contemporary Serious music and contemporary Popular music, including jazz. This curious obduracy in the face of acknowledged virtues stems, I think, from the persistence of an obsolete terminology. We regard the distinction between Serious and Popular as qualitative when it is, I believe, idiomatic. We are dealing, in my view, not with two grades, the one substantial and the other trivial, but with two separate musical idioms, the one European, the other Afro-American. Of that, more later.

But assuming, for the moment, the validity of this proposition, I remain, musically, a European, despite my affection and esteem for the Afro-American idiom, just as I remain a Philadelphian in my personal attitudes and speech despite nearly half a mature lifetime spent in central Europe. My early enthusiasms were opera and the symphony orchestra. My early idols were Kreisler, Rachmaninoff, Heifetz, Gabrilówitsch, Caruso, McCormack, Stracciari, DeLuca, Martinelli, Gigli, Lauri-Volpi and Ponselle.

All my schooling has been in their tradition; and their music, *i.e.*, the music of the European masters, is still the only music that I can play or sing. I listen to Sinatra and Fitzgerald, themselves airborne on the buoyant pulse of our own American music, with admiration and envy. I too would like to fly; but my wings were clipped long ago by a conventional musical pedagogy, concentrated vocally on the German *Lied*. Although American by birth and upbringing, I am, musically speaking—and above all rhythmically speaking—an earthbound German.

This is also the music in which I am most at home as listener and critic. Among jazz musicians, jazz critics and jazz fans I shall forever be a visitor from another realm—although I have always been made to feel welcome as a friend and fellow enthusiast. As a visitor, however, I have enjoyed some of the benefits and privileges reserved to the visitor in all walks of life. Free from the tedium and habits of routine, and unconcerned with local factions and parochial strife, the visitor regards the scene from a distance and with a certain detachment.

I am, musically speaking, a man without a country; but at the same time one whose country is everywhere. Certainly I cannot believe that good music is limited to the opera house, the concert hall and the recital room. I have heard it in other and more convivial places, and from many other kinds of musician. Good music, I believe, is where you find it, and he who confines his experience to one special school of music, to one specific idiom, even to as grand and rich an idiom as that which flourished in western Europe from the seventeenth century to the twentieth, not only impoverishes his pleasure but also, I suspect, inhibits his perception of the music of his own time.

The Schism

Two LITTLE WORDS, *serious* (or *classical*) and *popular*, in music today divide the essentially indivisible, frustrating communication and understanding among those whose common bond is the presumably universal language of music.

Art and *entertainment* might reflect more accurately the dichotomy of Western music in our century; for *popular*, as employed by most people, refers to anything from the Modern Jazz Quartet to Lawrence Welk, and within this world of Popular music there exists a series of sub-dichotomies, each modeled on the *serious-popular*, or *art-entertainment*, prototype. The jazz musician, for instance, sees a qualitative distinction between his own music and other music which he describes as commercial or popular; and even within the so-called pop groups, "commercial," which means "popular," is a dirty word.

The substitution of *art* for *serious* and *entertainment* for *popular* would point up, also, a fundamental paradox of contemporary esthetics implicit in the fact that so much of what we think of as *art* originated in an impulse to *entertain*—to divert, to amuse, to console, to move, to give plea-

29

sure. In music, which is essentially nonverbal, probably more than in literature or the graphic arts, the solemnity of so much that has survived tends to distort our notion of what constitutes worthy aspiration. We are solemn even in our assessment of the obviously lighthearted. One speaks, Calvinistically, of *mere* entertainment.

There has always been, in music, *für Jeden Etwas*—something for everyone. But not until our own time have the differences in how we approach music, and in what we expect from it, been reflected in separate, distinct, and mutually exclusive musical idioms. This would appear to be true *only* of music. A distinction is made between art and entertainment in other fields, however ill-advisedly; but the line is less sharply drawn. Only in music is the separation felt to be generic. There is Serious music, and there is Popular music, and the tendency of Popular musicians to divide their own music into Serious and Popular categories is simply the echo of a far more fundamental dichotomy.

The acknowledgment of a generic distinction, implicit in the employment of distinctive musical languages, is something new in the evolution of Western music. Time was—and it was no more than fifty years ago—when the language of music was, within the confines of the Western world, universal. To put it more precisely, all Western music spoke the same language. Some music may have had higher aspirations. Some music may have appealed to a more sophisticated audience. But all music had the same basic vocabulary.

Franz Liszt and all the other composer-virtuosos of his era flourished from potpourri arrangements of popular tunes, most of them from popular operas by Rossini, Donizetti, Pacini, Bellini, Weber, Meyerbeer, and even Mozart, Wagner and Verdi. Serious artists were still composing, playing and singing popular music well into this century, catering to the

30

tastes of a large and relatively unsophisticated audience. Some of us can remember when John McCormack, Caruso, Schumann-Heink, Kreisler, Cortot, Rachmaninoff and Tauber performed, in their recitals and on records, music, sometimes of their own composition, that is regarded today as beneath the dignity of a Serious musician.

This was still true of such younger artists as John Charles Thomas, Richard Crooks, Lawrence Tibbett and Ezio Pinza; but they all lived to see it rather counted against them. Furthermore, what they thought of as popular music was no longer so popular. The new household names were Bing Crosby, Frank Sinatra, Louis Armstrong, Duke Ellington, Benny Goodman, the Dorsey brothers and Artie Shaw, whose music differed from music congenial to the Serious musician not only in character but, more importantly, in idiom. The Serious performer ignored it not because he did not wish to sing it or play it but because he could not. With the Serious singer, even the songs of the musical theater, closer than jazz to his own music, found him ill at ease. Everyone, of course, could execute the notes, but they could not execute them idiomatically. And Ezio Pinza, for example, for all the thousands of times he sang "Some Enchanted Evening," was never at ease with its lilting rhythm and was dependent upon a conductor for rhythmic guidance.

Musical notation is, after all, no more than a system of symbols, and it is satisfactory only so long as the meaning or significance of the symbols is a matter of common agreement. Our Western musical notation has evolved from the conventions of musical performance in Europe over a span of roughly a thousand years. Everyone concerned in the performance of Serious music knows what is meant by the notes, rests, tempo and dynamics indicators, expression marks, key signatures, phrase contours, pedal markings, and so on.

Until the advent of jazz there was no fundamental confusion. But jazz originated with musicians who were, initially, and with some exceptions, musically illiterate; and it remained, for some time, an unwritten music. When, with wider dissemination and increasing literacy among the musicians, the time came to write it down, so that others could see, as well as hear on records, what an individual or a group had done, the European system of notation was used. But the symbols, aside from the designation of pitch, no longer meant quite the same things. Even pitch, because of the jazz musician's habit of slurring, could not always be shown precisely; and while the jazz musician would abide by a basic four beats to the measure, he would distort the time value of the notes within the measure in accordance with his own habits and conventions of phrasing and accentuation.

The conventional symbols could, in other words, indicate in a general way *what* should be played, but they could not indicate *how* it should be played. The jazz musician, reared in exotic conventions of performance, translated the symbols according to a new approach to melodic contour and pulse. And then he devised his own supplementary symbols to indicate to other jazz musicians the desired performance effects. To the Serious musician these new symbols were unintelligible; nor could he interpret the old symbols in accordance with the new jazz practice.

The idiomatic unity, which had made it possible for the greatest composers to write popular music and for the greatest performers to play it and sing it, was gone. The syntax and grammar of Serious music were no longer rooted in a contemporary vernacular. Never again could there be a Brahms "Lullaby," a "Melody in F," a *"Clair de Lune,"* a *"Träumerei"* or a "Prelude in C-sharp Minor." There was Serious music, almost all of it European and, in its contemporary manifestations, still dominated by Europeans and European concepts. And there was Popular music, primarily American, however widely imitated abroad, derived from a curiously haphazard fusion of Euro-American and African sources, and still dominated by Americans, including, very prominently, black Americans.

Nor was it simply that the Serious musician could no longer play or sing Popular music. The Popular musician, too, was idiomatically circumscribed; it was not possible for him to work his way up the social and artistic ladder to a position of respectability—unless, of course, he chose to switch idioms. No matter how great his genius, or how splendid his accomplishment, he was, as long as he played jazz, or something like it, a Popular musician. And by the early 1930s almost all Popular music reflected the influence of jazz. Thus categorized, the Popular musician was a victim of idiomatic segregation, condemned to second-class citizenship in a society never weary of trumpeting its democracy and its enlightened advocacy of *new* music.

Everyone sensed, of course, that jazz was exceptional. But since its origins were plebeian, and Negro plebeian at that, and since the white community first became aware of it as a music for dancing, every assessment of it was governed by habits of evaluation in a social context. Not even its own practitioners, initially at least, thought of jazz as anything but irretrievably lowbrow. The jazz-oriented Popular musician, not questioning his inferior status but seeking to improve it, wrote "up" to symphonic music, while the Serious composer, secure in his status but attracted by a vigorous primitive, wrote "down" to jazz.

George Gershwin, Ferde Grofé, Morton Gould and Duke Ellington on the one hand, and Stravinsky, Křenek and Milhaud on the other, thirty and forty years ago, attempted

33

to blend the two idioms in jazz suites, symphonies, concertos and operas. Every one of these early attempts at musical matchmaking foundered on the assumption that jazz might be susceptible of esthetic elevation and social improvement by exposure to a symphonic environment and the injection of blue symphonic blood. In the event, jazz, well-bred, was a bore; and a symphony orchestra trying to swing was about as edifying as an elderly patrician attempting the twist.

More recent efforts to achieve an accommodation have recognized the idiomatic distinction; and such composers as Rolf Liebermann and Dave Brubeck's brother Howard have been at pains, in their respective jazz concertos, to preserve it, choosing a kind of *concerto grosso* form in which the jazz ensemble is set off against a symphonic counterpart. Or, like Gunther Schuller, they have imagined a possible confluence in a music to which the term "third stream" attributes a livelier current than has ever been made apparent.

Characteristic of every attempt at juxtaposition and consolidation has been the failure, or the reluctance, of those concerned to grasp, or to acknowledge, the extent and the depth of the rift. It is not just a matter of idiomatic distinction. There is an audience distinction, too. The association of Serious music and jazz in the *concerto grosso* form is technically and even artistically possible. But it is not, therefore, necessarily desirable or satisfactory. The Serious-music audience, with rare exceptions, does not like jazz, and even the exceptional prefer to savor their diverse enthusiasm separately.

The two idioms—the Serious, or European, and the jazz, or Afro-American—are felt to be incompatible even by those with a taste for both; and this incompatibility goes beyond the specifics of composition and performance. The idioms are so far apart in origin, background, environment, practice, customs, habitat, aspiration, character, manner and technique that the adherents of the one—allowing, again, for a bilingual minority—cannot understand even the spoken language employed by the other's adherents to describe the music they know and love.

When we who have grown up in the world of Serious music talk about what we hear in Serious music, be it old or new, there is, as a rule, no uncertainty as to what we are talking about. The facts, the problems, the objectives, the styles, the individual artists and even the techniques are commonly recognized and satisfactorily identified, however variously they may be interpreted and assessed. It is possible to exchange views within a frame of reference of associations, expectations, purposes, forms and technical terms commonly accepted and commonly understood.

But if I, proceeding from my view of music as the lyrical extension of the melodic contours and cadences of speech and the rhythmic impulses of dance, look for the music of today that fulfills this function, and find it in jazz and the related world of American Popular music, I can rarely share the experience with my friends from the world of Serious music. We are no longer on common ground, or even on mutually familiar terrain. We grope for one another in a treacherous tangle of associations, concepts, terms, objectives, sentiments and experiences no longer shared or mutually understood.

It is not simply that my friends have not heard what I have heard, although this is often the case and obviously inhibits any fruitful exchange. Even hearing it, they will have listened with expectations conditioned by their experience of European music. They look and listen for something rooted in what they already know. Distressed, or offended, by the absence of characteristics they are accustomed to associate with "good music," and put off by much that impresses them as alien, they simply walk away and put it out of their heads, reminding me of the type of layman who dismisses Bach because "it all sounds alike."

The alien element, I suspect, can hardly be overestimated. Exoticism is all very well, even attractive, in the music of India, Indonesia, China or Japan. But it is something else again when it flourishes within one's own society. What Robert Ardrey has termed so felicitously the "territorial imperative" comes into play. The reaction of those who feel challenged is to close ranks and expel the intruder. Or, expulsion failing, to ignore, to exclude, to delimit, to isolate and to denigrate. All this has been characteristic of the Serious-music community's reaction to jazz. And it was probably inevitable.

For when we talk about American Popular music, whether it be jazz or any of the countless jazz derivatives, we are speaking of a music that has evolved outside the continuity of a Western, and hitherto European, musical evolution. We are speaking of a music with its own folklore and tradition, its own environment, its own history and aspirations, its own schedules of evaluation, its own instruments and instrumentation—or, at least, its own way of playing and combining the inherited instruments—as well as its own masters, its own critical fraternity, its own factions and its own descriptive terminology.

The circumstances of its origin—in the Negro slums of New Orleans and the back country of the American South—and the banality of its earliest diffusion throughout the white community in the Dixieland and white dance bands of the 1920s prompted the spokesmen of Serious music—composers, performers, critics and educators—to dismiss it as juvenile and inferior and, consequently, to ignore it, or, at best, to patronize it as an indigenous urban folk music. This attitude has survived a forty years' accumulation of evidence of its superficiality.

Typical is this amalgam of sarcasm, unctuous approbation and avuncular disparagement achieved by Aaron Copland in *The New York Times Magazine* of March 13, 1955, prompted by the publication of *The Agony of Modern Music:*

The juxtaposition of "jazz" and "classical" has been going on for a long time. I can remember it as an amusing vaudeville act when I was a boy. No one took it seriously then, and there is no reason why it should be taken seriously now. Certainly what our popular composers have accomplished is a source of pride to all of us. Anyone who has heard American jazz played for an audience in a foreign country, as I have, can testify to its enormous appeal. But to imagine that serious music is endangered by the wide acceptance of our popular music, or that one may be substituted for the other, is to be utterly naïve as to comparative musical values.

Precisely the same point of view was reflected by Paul Henry Lang in a discussion of *Porgy and Bess* in the *New York Herald Tribune* of January 29, 1956. Lang was deploring the fact that *Porgy and Bess* is widely accepted by laymen at home and abroad as an example of American music. Foreign audiences, he wrote, are given to understand that Gershwin represents our musical art in the same sense that Milhaud represents France's or Vaughan Williams England's.

No one can deny [he wrote] Gershwin's very real gifts, nor does anybody admit in public the limitations of those gifts and the fact that his music is exceptionally high quality Broadway show-music rather than "serious art." . . . The very fact that we use the rather silly-sounding terms, "serious" or "classical" music,

37

indicates that we do acknowledge the existence of some difference, and that we somehow assign a higher artistic value to, say, a symphony by Riegger or Piston than to, say, *Rhapsody in Blue* or *Showboat.*

It does—unfortunately and perversely. A classification born of quality retains a qualitative implication for anything now written under its emblem. A symphony by Wallingford Riegger or Walter Piston or Roger Sessions is better than a suite by Ellington or a musical by Gershwin simply because it is—a symphony! The Serious composer qualifies for respectability and status not on the basis of his accomplishment but merely through his choice of idiom.

The Serious-music critics and the Serious composers persistently and consistently confuse objective and accomplishment, inclination and talent. Their criteria are primarily categorical. Lang dismisses a work of "exceptionally high quality" because it is "Broadway show music" rather than "serious art." He dismisses *Rhapsody in Blue* because it is by Gershwin, a composer of Broadway show music, and despite the fact that it happens to be the most popular piano concerto since Rachmaninoff's in C minor. And this goes unchallenged because Lang's and Copland's view of jazz and its derivatives is widely shared in the Serious-music community, and because the Serious-music community is, in its professional echelons, the musical Establishment.

One might have expected a warmer welcome for *Rhapsody in Blue* and *Showboat,* and it might just have been accorded them had they not proved so overwhelmingly popular with the extensive outer, less doctrinaire fringe of the Serious-music audience. Both *Rhapsody in Blue* and *Showboat* are deferential to European forms and concepts—so much so, indeed, that the world of jazz disowns them. But the Serious-music community draws little comfort from their popularity with a public it would like to claim as its own. They are a convenience when benefit concerts require a numerous non-subscription audience. But there is still enough of the alien idiom in them to raise hackles. Johann Strauss and Lehár, yes. But Gershwin, Kern, Porter and Rodgers, no!

Beyond, or beneath, all these more or less musical considerations, obtuse and muddled as they may be, lies a more fundamental social incompatibility. Serious music is *dignified*. It is the symphony orchestra, opera in foreign languages, sonatas and concertos and string quartets, solemnly executed by solemn gentlemen from the universities and from Budapest and Amsterdam and Vienna and Paris. It is white tie and tails and Miss This and Mr. That and Madame So-and-so— and Maestro! It is a survivor of an Old World that is expiring rapidly, even in the Old World. Exposed to the brash music and the casual deportment of the jazz musician, the Serious-music community reacts with distaste. The saxophone, says the eminent accompanist, Gerald Moore, in his memoir *Am I Too Loud?* (1962), "is incapable of producing other than ignoble sounds."

What is one to make of *musicians* who are called King, Duke, Count, Earl, Smack, Cat, Fats, Muggsy, Dizzy, Bird, Monk, Bags, Rabbit, Bud, Lockjaw, Satchmo, Sweets, Cootie, Pinetop, Pres, Jelly Roll, Hawk, Leadbelly, Fatha, Chu, Baby, Buck, Lion, Bix, Woody, Zoot, Hot Lips, Ziggy and so on? This is not the type of moniker, certainly, that one is accustomed to associate with Art.

The vernacular terminology is similarly exotic, and, to the Serious musician, similarly appalling. An engagement is a gig. The familiar tune is a standard. A new composition is an original. An arrangement is a chart. A repertoire is a book. A style is a bag. Approbation is expended in such homely encomiums as swinging, groovy, wailing and cooking. A tempo indication may be written as "in a relaxed bop groove," or "medium-up" or "moderate walk with lay-back feeling." A dull musician, a dull piece, or a dull audience is a drag. The uninitiated are squares. Anything very good is a gas. To understand and to like is to dig. And the reluctant or recalcitrant are urged to get with it.

The musicians are cats. A record is not made; it is cut, or waxed. During a rest, the players, ungrammatically, "lay out." A chamber group is a combo. The members of a band are sidemen. A musician does not play an instrument; he is "on" it. His instrument is an "ax," and he "blows" it whether it is a horn or not. A visiting musician doesn't join in or participate; he sits in. A free lance is a studio man.

Nor are the titles of the pieces they play prepossessing. There are, of course, the familiar titles of popular tunes, not all of them edifying. And jazz musicians have a habit of contriving outlandish puns on their own names as titles of originals, with such consequences as "Carvin' the Bird" (Parker), "Bass-ically Speaking" (Basie) and "Hodgepodge" (Johnny Hodges). Or they go in for highfalutin titles such as "Ornithology," "Serendipity" and "Anthropology." One hopes that the peak was reached with Charles Mingus's "Pithecanthropus Erectus."

Finally, there are the places where jazz flourishes—or used to flourish: nightclubs, cabarets, musical bars and dance halls, all presumably disreputable. And the audience! Young people who chew gum, smoke, tap their feet, pop their fingers and applaud in the middle of a number, just as audiences used to do in Mozart's time. Surely, the Serious musician or critic will tell you, a music associated with such vulgar terminology and environment cannot be a threat to composition dedicated to perpetuating the traditions of Bach, Beethoven and Brahms!

The more knowledgeable may concede the vitality of jazz; they may applaud and envy its spontaneity and admire the virtuosity and improvisatory genius of its outstanding professionals. But the Serious-music community, whether it listens with admiration or distaste, or with a mixture of both, thinks of jazz as *popular,* as essentially and generically inferior; and the mere suggestion that it should be taken seriously, that it might be thought of as a cultural ornament, as a form of music on an equal footing with the music of Stravinsky, Berg, Webern, Hindemith, Britten, Sessions, Barber, Messaien, Boulez or Berio, is to open a Pandora's box of outrage, indignation and denunciation.

One is accused immediately of equating commercial success with artistic quality, the implication being that everything conventionally classified as Popular is commercially successful, which it isn't, and that commercial success and artistic quality are mutually exclusive, which they aren't. One is accused of accepting the Hit Parade and the Top Forty as infallible arbiters of artistic achievement, although little of the music that we are talking about ever appears on either. One is accused, finally, of committing our musical culture to the dictates of the jukebox and the disc jockeys, about which the jazz community has rarely been heard to utter a friendly sound.

The most common technique of counterattack consists in setting up the most advantageous juxtapositions. One contrasts the Hit Parade or the Top Forty with the St. Matthew Passion or the Ninth Symphony and returns in triumph to the ivory tower. It matters little that the victory is irrelevant and fraudulent, that in contrasting the best of the eighteenth and early nineteenth centuries with what may be the worst of

41

the twentieth one is evading the issue. It is possible to turn the tables by comparing the best of Ellington and Basie, or the Modern Jazz Quartet, with the worst of Tchaikovsky, Grieg, Saint-Saëns and Dvořák. But this, too, is merely an evasion, a debater's gimmick.

The real issue lies elsewhere, remote and difficult of access, obscured by the age-old conventions of our historical and esthetic approach to European music. Not everyone in Serious music is hidebound. There are those who recognize and appreciate the exceptional accomplishments of American songwriters, composers, arrangers, singers and jazz instrumentalists but who fail to find in even the best of their music the same spiritual and intellectual substance that so distinguished the masterpieces of European music.

One may argue that this substance is also lacking in Serious music of the past fifty years; and most Serious music critics and Serious composers would agree that this is true, as it is also true of contemporary painting, sculpture and literature as compared with the European, British and Russian masterworks of the past.

But contemporary composers of Serious music, like the writers and graphic artists, still aim at that substance, or profess to, and they are taken at their word and dealt with deferentially, however far they may appear to fall short of the objective. Their music is associated, at least, with the older masterworks as a matter of lineal descent and as the product of a traceable evolution. It comes of good stock, so to speak, and is accorded the privileges of recognition and indulgence associated with being well-born and enjoying good family connections.

In music, however, and in music alone, our understanding of what has happened in our century is confused by the injection of an alien culture and by the arrival of an art form

from an improbable quarter. In art and literature the assumed "modernity" of the contemporary product may well
be as bogus as I hold the "modernity" of contemporary Serious music to be. But neither in the graphic arts, nor in literature, is there a vital so-called subculture to disturb the
assumptions of an Establishment, although the pop-art phenomenon can be interpreted as a preemptive defense against
the skill and imagination of the commercial artist.

A discussion of what is modern in music, and what is not,
belongs to a subsequent chapter. It will suffice for the moment to concede that there is, indeed, something missing in
even the best American Popular music that leaves unsatisfied
the appetite of the music lover brought up on the European
masterpieces, and to argue rather that music can merit our
attention, our affection and respect without being like Beethoven, without associating itself with Faustian objectives,
and without being able to point to an uninterrupted European bloodline.

Missing from much of jazz is the *leisurely* buildup of
tension that European music achieves—or once achieved—
through modulatory structure, thematic development,
change of pace and the adding of instruments. Climaxes, in
European music, could be prepared over a longer span of
time and cover a wider range of dynamics and color. Tension
in jazz tends to be constant, working upward from a fairly
high mean.

This is attributable, in part, at least, to the circumstances
in which jazz is played and heard. In nightclubs, cabarets,
bars and dance halls, the musician must compete with such
other diversions as eating, drinking, chatter and dancing, and
with such mundane disturbances as the happy ringing of the
cash register, the movement of waiters and bartenders, and
the arrival and departure of guests. Even in jazz concerts

there is the problem of holding the attention of large assemblies of young people in huge places. The jazz musician is denied the luxury of the Serious musician's disciplined and docile audience, and he must gauge his performance accordingly.

But there are technical limitations, also, to the tensile range and variety of jazz. The prevailing variation form, while it facilitates thematic elaboration, conspires against the discursive kind of thematic development that is native to the multi-thematic sonata form. And in the AABA form common to most American song writing, the B element, usually a mere eight measures, is too short to permit more than a suggestion of dramatic or pictorial contrast. The basic twelve-bar form of the blues is even more restrictive in terms of expansive thematic development. Jazz achieves its contrasts dynamically, and builds its climaxes expeditiously.

Translated into language more readily accessible to the layman, this all adds up to a deficiency in jazz of that indefinable something that we think of as "romantic" in the nineteenth-century German sense. Jazz is not wanting, certainly, in eloquence and intensity of emotional utterance; but it tends to be explicit, direct, straight to the point, abjuring nineteenth-century predilections for contemplation, reflection, introspection, doubt, misgiving and ambivalence, to say nothing of long-windedness. It must forgo certain refinements that European music derived from the strings, horns and woodwinds, and from the flexible tempos of a recitative style. When jazz compromises its own characteristic directness and assertiveness, its own conceptions of pulse, contour and cadence, to accommodate a more nearly European frame of expressive reference, calling upon strings, or employing its own European instruments in a European manner, it jeopardizes its idiomatic identity.

44

The absence of strings in jazz is symptomatic, and also, probably, the absence of the oboe, one of the most thoughtful and reflective of the instruments of the symphony orchestra. There is simply something about these instruments—and about the English horn and the bassoon, too—that does not lend itself to twentieth-century candor. Even the avant-garde composers of Serious music often seem at a loss as to what to do with strings. They dare not do without them, for the strings are inseparable from the European tradition; and so the composers commonly choose to abuse them rather than dispense with them.

The element of mystery, the sense of otherworldliness, the suggestion of communication with an Infinite, the pattern of conflict between good and evil, God and man, the concept of the individual's struggle with himself and his environment, all characteristic of the German masterpieces of the nineteenth century—Beethoven, Schubert, Schumann, Brahms, Wagner, Strauss, Bruckner, Mahler and even Schoenberg and Berg—all this is foreign to jazz, as it is also to most twentieth-century Serious music. The catch is that jazz, for reasons suggested previously, is faulted, while Serious contemporary music is not.

Other arguments introduced by the European-oriented to demonstrate that jazz is generically and intrinsically inferior may be dealt with more briefly and less sympathetically. Among them are complaints of harmonic poverty and rhythmic monotony; and they do the plaintiffs no credit. Those who speak disdainfully of the harmonic element in jazz are plainly unaware of what has been going on for the past twenty years; while those who complain of rhythmic monotony have not got beyond the basic beat to hear what goes on around it.

Suggestions of intellectual inferiority are, in my opinion,

very suspect. Intellect and musical talent constitute a precari-ous partnership. Music is not an art of the intellect, and its greatest practitioners, while intelligent, as a rule, have rarely been intellectuals. European music grew steadily more intel-lectual during the nineteenth century, to be sure—Wagner, especially, having been a kind of intellectual monster—but this may well be considered a symptom of its decline.

Intellect is, unfortunately, inseparable from self-conscious-ness. When a music becomes self-conscious it has lost its innocence. And when it has lost its innocence it has also lost one of its essential and affective attributes. Jazz, too, has lost its innocence in the past twenty years—with consequences that belong to a later chapter. But the American Popular idiom, of which jazz, however defined, is only one of many styles, continues to be fed from innocent sources, and thus it continues, for the time being, at least, to survive as a living art.

For the time being—there lies, it seems to me, a clue to what I have described earlier as remote and difficult of access. The spokesmen of the Serious-music community assess jazz in the light of traditional European esthetic conventions as if these were forever immutable. In noting what appear to them to be the deficiencies and inadequacies of American Popular music in general, and of jazz in particular, they persistently ignore the passage of time. They speak glibly of the European masterpieces as immortal. I find this a hazard-ous, even foolhardy, assumption.

The most ancient of this music is hardly more than three hundred and fifty years old. Very little of what is still heard is as old as that, and even that little represents a tiny percentage of a vast output that was once as fully alive as American Popular music is today. Most of the standard repertoire is very much younger; and it, too, represents only a puny

46

portion of the music of its own time. To believe that it will live forever is characteristic of the kind of historical perspective in which a mere century appears as eternity.

The life span of a musical masterpiece may encompass a number of generations; but music, being a reflection of society, is subject, like any other art, to social obsolescence. It may endure, metaphorically speaking, in libraries, on records and in the occasional archeological revival. But it will not satisfy forever a changing society's changing musical requirements.

What one derives from a musical composition or performance depends upon the kind of receptivity one brings to it. With those masterpieces of the nineteenth century, particularly, in which are concentrated the musical attributes most readily identifiable as foreign to jazz, and which constitute the core of the Serious-music repertoire, the listener's receptivity must include a predisposition to go along with their assumed subjective and picturesque content, to accept a sense of meaning, of significance, of intellectual, dramatic, graphic and philosophical substance. The suggestion of ideational content, of message and image, is the distinctive characteristic of this music; and it is also its most conspicuous vulnerability.

For this subject matter is intangible and, even in program music, incapable of definitive verbal elucidation; it is nothing more, indeed, than imaginative association, either voluntary or induced by the reading of program notes. Our forefathers reveled in this kind of inferential listening, untroubled by the fact that no two of them ever drew the same inferences, and resentful of the Hanslicks and Kalbecks, who took a bemused view of their imaginings as reminiscent of the visions of opium eaters.

Our contemporary Serious composers do not favor this kind of associative listening; and they rarely cater to it. A reaction set in shortly after the turn of the century, and in this, at least, the composer was reflecting the spirit of the time. His misfortune was that he did not reflect the spirit of the Serious-music audience, the greater part of which has remained, well into the twentieth century, a monumental relic of the nineteenth—on its knees and gazing upward, transfixed, into a Valhalla inhabited by Handel, Bach, Haydn, Mozart, Beethoven, Schubert, Schumann, Brahms, Wagner, Strauss, Mahler and Bruckner.

Nor did the Serious composer go far enough to reach a significantly wider and more representative audience. Other listeners found in various manifestations of the American Popular idiom a music more contemporary in spirit and style than neoclassical objectivism or dodecadogmatic abstraction. And the composer reckoned, too, without the tenacious longevity of the German masters. They are mortal, surely, but they have already outlived him.

It is simply a fact of musical life today that hundreds of thousands of music lovers in Europe (including the Soviet Union), the United Kingdom, North and South America and Australia still think of music and its pleasures in terms of European music, most of it German and almost all of it German-influenced. It is this music that most people have in mind when they speak of "good music," using the term generically, and untroubled in their colloquial employment of the qualifying adjective by the knowledge that some of it may be, even in their own assessment, not very good.

How long this will continue to be so is another matter. Fifty or a hundred years, possibly, although with today's multiplicity of public performance and recording of a few hundred standard classics the span may well be shorter within which the masterpieces will cease to mean what they once did, or what they mean to many people now. With so much

48

vested interest involved, however, there can be no doubt that existence will be prolonged through artificial respiration by art councils, foundations, universities and national, state and municipal subsidies.

We now have, in any case, what some have called a bifurcation of musical life. Those who so use the term are thinking, of course, of a permanent division of music into *art* or *serious* music on the one hand and *popular* or *commercial* music on the other. And this is comforting to those who sense a threat in any suggestion that the high quality of the best of American Popular music, and the exceptional achievements of the musicians concerned with it, entitle it to be taken seriously. I tend to think of this bifurcation as temporary, destined to endure only so long as the European masterpieces retain their capacity to nourish the musical requirements of a numerous contemporary public.

The decisive fact is the failure of *contemporary* Serious music to nourish and satisfy that appetite. And with fifty years having elapsed since the composition of Schoenberg's *Erwartung,* it is no longer unreasonable to speak of failure. Indeed, it is hardly reasonable not to do so. The American Popular idiom, in the meantime, has embraced an even more numerous, worldwide public, no less discriminating among its more sophisticated membership, for whom this music offers nourishment rich in the rewards of artistic experience.

The transitional phase may already be farther advanced than we think, as evidenced by the number of younger musicians who have switched idioms or who have found it possible and expedient to be conversant with each. The older symphony orchestra musician, chamber musician, instrumental virtuoso and opera singer are, to be sure, rarely among them, notable exceptions being the Austrian pianist Friedrich Gulda and the American conductor-composer-jazz

49

pianist André Previn. Nor are the most dedicated of the jazz musicians able, as a rule, to live in any other atmosphere than their own.

But the amphibious, so to speak, are now a commonplace among the younger musicians working in the recording studios. Many young composers, including the conservatory-trained, are slipping off into the promising fields of motion-picture and TV-serial underscore writing, where both idioms may be employed according to the requirements of period and subject matter. And young composers and arrangers reared in the American idiom find it possible and fruitful to master the traditional techniques, procedures and conventions.

Similarly, while the symphony-orchestra, concert-series and opera-subscription audience may continue to be uniformly European-oriented, the same does not hold true of the enormous public that buys and collects records, many of whom have come to music through an initial fascination with the science and mechanics of high fidelity. Their tastes are less tradition-bound, their choices more eclectic and more catholic, uninhibited by conventional schooling and attitudes, uncontaminated by the parochialism of music appreciation. Their listening habits are likely to embrace both worlds, and the many varieties of each.

The typical Serious-music lover knows little or nothing of all this; and chances are that the older among them will never learn. They deny themselves the pleasure and excitement of participation in a truly contemporary music, but what they don't know won't hurt them. And they have one conspicuous advantage. They know with absolute certainty—or think that they do—what their music is. The American Popular or jazz musician and music lover do not. Or, if one of them thinks he does, he finds no consensus in his own community.

Classical—
Jazz—Popular

WHAT IS JAZZ?

Professional musicians of all categories, and many lay enthusiasts, have been wrestling with this question for half a century, and no one has yet achieved a commonly acceptable answer, jazz musicians themselves least of all. But until a commonly acceptable answer is found, we shall remain in the dark about the evolution of Western music in the twentieth century.

The best way to begin, it seems to me, is to seek a factual starting point. And almost everyone, I think, including the most exclusively disposed jazz musicians and jazz critics, would accept the following formulation as a serviceable fact:

The influence of a variety of indigenous musical styles originating in the Negro communities of New Orleans and other American cities, in the Negro communities of the rural South, and in the Negro or mixed communities of the Caribbean Islands and some areas of South America in the early decades of the twentieth century has been felt and reflected in the popular music of most of the civilized world.

But no one would argue, surely, that all the music covered by this generalization is jazz, nor would any two persons agree on what part of it is jazz. The source of the confusion is not just the infinite variety of musical styles that reflect the influence of jazz, nor even the successive phases of jazz—New Orleans, Dixieland, swing, bop, cool, progressive, and now avant-garde—each of which, in turn, has been denounced by some jazz musicians and jazz enthusiasts as "not the real jazz." It is rather the jazz musician's inability to formulate any satisfactory definition of precisely what it is that sets jazz off from its own commercial derivatives. In his quest of acceptance and status he is the victim of his own musical vitality. There is no comfort for him in the old cliché about imitation being the highest form of compliment. Imitation, to him, is a pain in the neck, exposing him to evaluations based on what he himself views as a debasement of his art.

The Serious musician, conversely, in the security of his status, benefits from his own obsolescence. His idiom no longer has a vulgar by-product to disturb an image of artistic integrity and cultural chastity. Its heritage is felt, to be sure, in all Popular music, including every variety of jazz; and the worst Popular music is, as a rule, the most European in its antecedents—or was until rock 'n' roll came along. But the Afro-American idiom, whether predominant or not, is so distinctive that jazz, rather than Serious music, is thought of as the idiomatic source, and no one thinks of associating Popular music with Serious music.

During its natural lifetime, *i.e.,* until shortly after the turn of the century, the European idiom produced vast quantities of Popular music, more of it bad than good, and the worst of it fully as bad as the worst that the Afro-American idiom produces today. But all that is dead and forgotten now, and only the masterpieces remain. Jazz, on the other hand, having been both a Popular music and a source of Popular music, is continually embarrassed with unflattering distortions of its own image. It is the price that the jazz musician has to pay for having fathered a truly contemporary music.

Try as he will to throw off the Popular label, to dissociate himself from commercially viable derivatives, he cannot do it. The relationship is there, sufficiently discernible in the unprepossessing physiognomy of much Popular music to frustrate any denial of kinship. His own relative popularity has been his undoing, inspiring imitation, emulation and adaptation by those who think of popularity in terms not of hundreds of thousands but of tens of millions.

He is aware, of course, of an idiomatic distinction between his own and Serious music, and he acknowledges it, deferentially, by referring to Serious music, colloquially, as "legit," a carry-over from the use of the same term to distinguish the living theater from the motion picture, and conveying the same self-deprecatory concession of a social and cultural priority to the older medium. But he has never been able to define this distinction; and until he can define it, he will be unable to define his own music and come to terms with his relationship to Popular music.

Failing this insight, he remains ill-equipped as a spokesman in his own behalf. He does not, to put it bluntly, know what he is talking about. This innocence inhibits him as a musician not at all; rather the contrary. He knows perfectly well what he is playing, and he knows how it should be played. But in terms of his quest of status his innocence is a catastrophe. His every attempt to correct what he regards, reasonably enough, as a common misconception of himself and his music only compounds the confusion. For no one is more confused than he.

At the root of all this misunderstanding and confusion is the fact that the most widely popular manifestations of jazz have almost always been a white dilution of a black original, *e.g.,* Dixieland as a derivative of New Orleans, swing as a derivative of the Negro dance bands of the 1930s, rock 'n' roll as a derivative of rhythm-and-blues, and, most recently, the pop groups as a derivative of the urban blues.

When most people talked about jazz in the 1920s and early 1930s, for example, they were thinking not about King Oliver and Louis Armstrong's Hot Five, but about Paul Whiteman, Vincent Lopez, Ben Bernie, Ted Lewis, Fred Waring, Guy Lombardo and Ted Weems, about the songs of Irving Berlin, Jerome Kern, Vincent Youmans and George Gershwin, and about the singing of Al Jolson, Ruth Etting and Harry Richman. Paul Whiteman was known in those days as the "King of Jazz."

One of the earliest books on jazz in the United States, Henry Osgood's *So This Is Jazz* (1926), did not mention the name of a single black musician. In a book on jazz today one will hardly find the names of Whiteman, Lopez, Bernie, Lewis, Weems or Waring, unless it is addressed specifically to that era, or unless the author is discussing some revered jazz musician who was so down on his luck that he was reduced to playing with them. Bix Beiderbecke's playing with Whiteman is the classic example. And yet it was the music of Whiteman and the other white band leaders that led to this period's being designated "the jazz age."

Few of the fans, in the following decade, who proclaimed Benny Goodman "the King of Swing," had heard, or were aware of, the earlier big bands of Duke Ellington, Cab Calloway, Jimmie Lunceford, Fletcher Henderson, Bennie Moten, Chick Webb or Count Basie, or knew that Goodman's principal arranger was Henderson and that Tommy Dorsey's was Sy Oliver, both Negroes. And even more recently, at the height of the rock 'n' roll craze, few of its enthusiasts have been aware of the parent rhythm-and-blues and urban blues.

In other words, while jazz criticism now tends to think of jazz in terms of two or three generations of superbly original black musicians in New Orleans, Kansas City, Chicago and New York, and of the white musicians most closely identified with them, the rest of the world, including the world of Serious music, has thought of jazz in terms of less conspicuously original, more readily assimilable, white derivatives in which European influences were more obviously and decisively at work.

There is confusion, too, about the functions of jazz. The jazz musician and the jazz critic do not think of jazz as dance music, nor do they want to. Admittedly, there is no dancing at jazz concerts, and none, as a rule, in musical bars and some nightclubs where jazz bands and jazz combos are the principal attraction. But the fact remains that all the great bands of jazz history, including those playing today, have played for dancing, and that most dance bands play jazz—or are popularly assumed to play jazz.

This, from the jazz musician's point of view, is a serious matter; for it exposes jazz to the fashionable prejudice against art as entertainment. The same inhibition applies to the musical materials of jazz. The jazz musicians and the jazz critics, dissociating their music from Popular music, do not consider Irving Berlin, Jerome Kern, George Gershwin, Harold Arlen, Cole Porter and other American songwriters as jazz musicians or composers; but it is impossible to deny that the American popular song, even more than the revered blues, has provided the jazz musician's basic melodic and harmonic materials. Not for nothing are the famous songs of these composers referred to in the terminology of jazz as "standards."

Jazz musicians and jazz critics know this. They know, too, that while any tune by any composer of any period can be played in the jazz manner, the songs of the American song-writer lend themselves to this treatment better than any others. They reflect the cadences of modern American speech, and they accommodate readily the distortions of rhythm and melodic contour characteristic of jazz. It would seem to follow, then, that the songwriter cannot be excluded from jazz. But the jazz musician will acquiesce only grudgingly or not at all; for the association links him to show business, commerce and entertainment, and threatens his integrity—according to the conventions of our time—as an Artist.

Confusion becomes chaotic when one discusses the people who sing these songs. Ella Fitzgerald, Sarah Vaughan and the late Billie Holiday, all Negro, are commonly accepted as jazz singers by jazz critics who, in the next breath, may be maintaining stoutly that jazz cannot be sung. These ladies, and particularly Fitzgerald and Vaughan, have all sung a great deal of music that the jazz musician thinks of as Popular rather than jazz, and they have sung it in a manner tailored to popular taste. But they have also been associated with some of the greatest jazz musicians, and they are listed under "Jazz" as well as "Popular" in the annual readers' polls in the jazz magazines.

The most instructive forum for the discussion of jazz by jazz musicians has long been Leonard Feather's "Blindfold Test" in *Down Beat,* in which musicians are asked to comment on records about which they are given no information. Their answers are tape-recorded. And they tell us all we need to know about the jazz musician's own confusion. Charles Mingus, for instance, had this to say about Oscar Peterson and Buddy de Franco: "No stars! Because this is supposed to be a jazz review, and I don't think that's jazz." And of Lee Konitz he said, "This makes me mad, because it's not jazz, and people are calling this kind of beat jazz. Dave Brubeck gets the same beat. . . . I think these cats hate jazz!" He was more kindly disposed toward Shelly Manne, of whom he observed, "Since he left Kenton he's found out what jazz is."

At about the same time that this interview occurred, one could read in *Down Beat's* competitor, *Metronome,* the same Shelly Manne (who now knew what jazz was) describing "the exciting exploration emanating from . . . Dave Brubeck," and Pete Rugolo (a Kenton arranger) speaking of Oscar Peterson "taking chorus after chorus, even on the blues, and really building, really getting somewhere."

Also in the same periodicals at that time, in the late 1950s, one could find Stan Kenton saying that the Glenn Miller band "was not a jazz band, ever!" and John S. Wilson, jazz critic of *The New York Times,* saying of Kenton, "Any view of the merit of his band is conditioned by the extent to which the listener will go along with Kenton's notion that either shrieking brass or dolorous solemnity is indicative of advanced jazz."

As late as 1967 a consensus was no nearer, as was demonstrated in a panel discussion at the University of California in Berkeley. Participants were pianist Bill Evans, modern saxophonist John Handy and critics Feather and Gleason. The following is extracted from Russ Wilson's report of the discussion in *Down Beat* June 15, 1967:

Evans said, "Jazz is a mental attitude rather than a style. It uses a certain process of the mind expressed spontaneously through some musical instrument. I'm concerned with retaining that process."

Feather brought up the matter of improvisation.

"I believe it is necessary to jazz," Evans commented.

"Then how about Lawrence Welk?" Gleason asked. "He had a clarinet player who improvised."

"Then he was playing jazz," Evans replied.

No one mentioned that the clarinetist was Pete Fountain, and that he finally quit Welk to form his own New Orleans-based combo.

Handy made the point that the spirit with which it is played has a good deal to do with jazz and went on to say it has influenced all kinds of music.

Evans agreed, but added "Because of jazz's wide influence some people are playing bad jazz."

Gleason posed the question, "If it's jazz when it's improvised, can it be jazz when it's not—that is, when it's written?"

"I'd say not," Evans answered.

Feather, however, cited the fact that orchestras such as Ellington's, Count Basie's and Gerald Wilson's utilize written music, yet the way and the spirit with which they play make it jazz. On the other hand, he said, "the music of the Middle East or India is improvised, but it's not jazz because it comes from a different culture."

The panelists finally decided there's no absolute definition for jazz.

There have always been the parochial dogmatists, of course, and they, at least, have been untroubled by doubt. There were, first, the "moldy figs" who washed their hands of swing and argued that jazz had sold its birthright when Louis Armstrong was encouraged to shatter the pattern of communal counterpoint by embarking on virtuoso solos. Other parochialists swallowed swing but drew the line at bebop, or bop. Among these was Hugues Panassié, the pioneer French jazz critic, who contributed the following to the 1954 edition of Grove's *Dictionary of Music and Musicians:*

Actually, bebop is considered as jazz neither by Louis Armstrong and other great jazz musicians, nor by most of the champions of bop themselves. The great difference between jazz and bebop is that the latter is devoid of the regular pulsating rhythm which is the generating force of swing. . . . Another important difference between these two kinds of music is that bebop soloists have broken with the instrumental tradition of the Negroes. They do not let their instruments sing like human voices. They learn the instrumental technique at the Juilliard School of Music in New York, a technique which is opposed to that of jazz. Furthermore, their improvisations are full of harmonic effects borrowed from modern European music. For these reasons, whatever may be thought of the musical value of bebop, it must be recognized that we have here no longer wholly Negro-inspired music, and it can therefore not legitimately be incorporated into jazz properly speaking, *which is the popular dance music of the black races of the U.S.A. and, in fact, their only genuine instrumental music.*

This concentrate of dubious opinion and misinformation was, at least, an improvement on Gerald Abraham's article in the 1940 supplement to the third (1927) edition, which described jazz as an "unrestrained Corybantic frenzy alternating with passive hopeless melancholy. . . . Rhapsodic improvisation by a solo player, or even several soloists simultaneously, plays a very important part in jazz performance. When this element predominates, the result is known as 'hot jazz.' "

Some who accepted bop were skeptical about cool—and remain skeptical to this day. Nat Hentoff, one of the most prolific of jazz critics, is among them. Attempting, in the June 29, 1967 issue of *Down Beat,* to rationalize the small audience for what *he* thinks of as jazz, he wrote: "From time to time, there have been mirages of a radically widening audience for jazz. The West Coast phenomenon of the 1950s, for instance. The Brubeck phenomenon. But that kind of music was tangential to jazz, and so were its audiences."

The pattern of rejection has been repeated, almost needless to say, with the New Jazz of the 1960s—Ornette Coleman, Albert Ayler, Archie Shepp, Charles Lloyd, etc. Some vivid comment will be recalled later, but the following, by Shelly Manne on Ayler in a Blindfold Test, is appropriate to the present context: "It's easy to play that way because you don't have to worry about swinging, don't have to create melody, don't have to adhere to any form, don't have to do anything except squawk on the horns. . . . It may be another kind of music that I don't want to have anything to do with. But it's not jazz. Not in any way, shape or form!"

Again and again one is confronted with the statement: "It's not jazz," and almost always in connection with a kind of music that is commonly thought of as jazz—even Dixieland! The pianist Billy Taylor, for example, a modernist by the conventions of the 1950s, but wide-ranging in his knowledge and enthusiasms, and certainly not a "moldy fig," writes in his booklet, "Dixieland Solos and How to Play Them": "Though it featured syncopation and some improvisation, Dixieland was not jazz. It was a new way of playing music, not a new music." Jazz, in other words, is not a new way of playing, but a new music.

A definitive clue? A few days after first reading Taylor, I turned to George Simon, a jazz critic whose career has covered every phase of jazz. Wasn't most Popular or commercial music, I asked, derived more or less from jazz? "Not at all," he said. "Jazz is not really a music. It's a way of playing." But it was Leonard Feather, I think, who observed at about this time, "Dixie has passed from the status of a specialized esoteric music into a new acceptance as popular music. . . . Similarly, one can hear swing music, such as the bands of the thirties provided, on any major TV show today." In other words, most Popular or commercial music *is* derived more or less from jazz.

This suggests a riddle: When is jazz not jazz? Answer: When it is Popular. Or, to put it in more musicological terms, jazz ceases to be jazz when its initially exotic characteristics are no longer felt as exotic, and when the style itself— New Orleans, Dixieland, swing, etc.—has been absorbed irrevocably in a musical vernacular.

This, it seems to me, opens up a workable vein. What the jazz musician really is up to, in his insistence that this or that kind of music is *not jazz,* is self-protection. He is jealous of his separate identity, which is jeopardized as soon as any new jazz style is swept up in the mainstream of Popular music. The poor fellow can't win. If the new style catches on, he is bound to be robbed. If it fails, its failure is his. This dilemma is the root of most recent jazz history.

Another way of saying the same thing, more pertinent to the pursuit of definition, is to suggest that the jazz musician uses "jazz" as a synonym for "good," reacting instinctively to the Serious-music community's preemption of "good" as a component of "good music." The best he can hope for is a categorical separation from Popular. And in this he has had some success. The mass magazines and newspapers, in their jazz columns, acknowledge the distinction. Signs on record store windows may read CLASSICAL-JAZZ-POPULAR. But it is only half a victory. The record magazines reflect the accounting more accurately, distinguishing jazz from Popular, but separating both jazz and Popular from Classical by lumping them, side by side, under Entertainment.

But just this arbitrary division should suggest to the jazz musician a more soundly based strategy. His struggle to escape the embrace of Popular music is self-destructive. Popular music is too much a part of him, and he too much a part of it. Instead of fighting Popular music, he should lead it. Instead of attempting to define jazz as a music separate and distinct from Popular music, which—as must be obvious by now—he cannot do, he should seek to establish just what it is that distinguishes *both* jazz and its Popular derivatives from Serious, or classical, music. This accomplished, he could then challenge the propriety of such prejudicial terminology as Classical and Entertainment. The distinction is there, all right. Only the nomenclature is wrong. It can be corrected only by a clearer insight into the nature of the division. And to achieve this insight should not be an insuperable task.

The objective, then, is to distinguish not between jazz and Popular, but between jazz and Serious; and the first step must be the clearing away of an accumulation of rubbishy opinion and superstition, not all of it, by any means, attributable solely to the Serious-music community's ignorance of the subject. Prevalent assumptions are: (1) that the distinguishing feature of jazz is syncopation; (2) that the distinguishing feature of jazz is improvisation; (3) that jazz cannot be played from notes; and (4) that jazz is a Negro music and can be played properly only by Negroes.

All are easily disposed of: (1) If syncopation were the distinctive element in jazz, then much European music would be jazz. (2) Improvisation was common in European music well into the nineteenth century, and most church organists improvise to this day without producing anything that sounds like jazz. (3) The time has long passed when an astigmatic jazz musician could get by without spectacles. (4) While the Negro has certainly been the decisive contributor to jazz, there is no jazz in Africa that was not brought there by Americans or Europeans, white, black and mixed.

Usually, and more sensibly, the distinction between jazz and Serious music is sought in rhythm, and there, I believe, is where it is to be found, although it will not show up in the written notes. In every other relevant respect jazz and Serious music are alike. The pitches and their arrangement in scales are the same, and they are similarly notated. The flatted third and the flatted seventh of jazz, in which some musicologists have identified a characteristically Negroid inflection, are not present in all jazz, nor are they necessarily alien to European music. Chords and tonal relationships are the same. Even compositional structure is the same, although jazz, in often elaborating upon a conventional thirty-two-bar melody, usually confines itself to the theme-and-variation form, or to a *chaconne*-like improvisation over the chords identified with the theme.

When jazz is written down, any Serious musician can read it and play it; *i.e.*, he can play the notes, and he can play them in the tempo indicated. But what he produces, unless he happens to be versed in both idioms, will not be jazz. This is not satisfactorily rationalized by the assumption that the jazz musician, playing the same notes in the same tempo, would add to them improvisationally, and that this element of improvisation would represent the difference between his performance and that of the Serious musician. The jazz musician could play the same notes without improvisation and still produce a fundamentally different music. The Serious musician could improvise and still not produce jazz.

The difference lies in *accentuation,* and this accentuation is rhythmically conditioned, even with both musicians playing in the same tempo and with the same four beats to the measure. Jazz is often described as a music of rhythm, and the jazz musician's superiority in his own idiom is attributed to his peculiar rhythmic sense. There is truth in this, although it still leaves much unexplained and unaccounted for. But let us return, for a moment, to our two musicians—pianists, if you like—and see what happens when each of them plays a piece of written-down jazz. And let us look as well as listen.

The eye will pick up immediately an important difference. The jazz musician will beat the rhythm with his foot. The Serious musician, not versed in jazz, will not.

To the Serious musician, this habit of beating time with the foot—or, for that matter, with the drum or double bass—is one of the offensive aspects of jazz, and it is the most difficult for him to assimilate. It seems to imply a want of rhythmic sensibility, certainly a lack of rhythmic subtlety, suggesting an elementary stage of musical development, or a beginner counting out loud. Sir Jack Westrup, Heather Professor of Music at Oxford, for instance, commenting on my *Death of a Music?* in the October 1961 issue of *Music and Letters,* the English counterpart of *The Musical Quarterly,* objected that the musician should not have to pronounce the beat in order to keep time. And Stanley Sadie, of the London *Times,* expressed a similar bias in his castigation of a certain pianist's performance of Beethoven's Concerto in C minor in the spring of 1967: "It might have been Czerny exercises—except that no decent teacher would allow a pianist to bang out the rhythm with her left foot."

The jazz musician's view is quite another. To him the *explicit* beat of jazz, as opposed to the *implicit* beat of most Serious music, is what sends him aloft and keeps him there. It supports his rhythmic, melodic and harmonic flight. He can be with it, ahead of it, behind it or against it. As long as it is there with him, and he with it—as long as his relationship to it is secure, easy and relaxed—he is, so to speak, musically airborne. If he were to lose contact with it, or come into uncontrolled conflict with it, he would plummet back to earth.

This, basically, is what is implied by the term *swing,* a more communicative word, certainly, than *jazz.* And it is a commonplace of jazz jargon that a musician who is thought to swing is considered a jazzman, and that one who does not swing is not. Swinging is, after all, a kind of flying; and the essence of jazz is musical flight, sustained by rhythmic pulsations and by tensions resulting from controlled rhythmic deviation.

This is more or less true, of course, of all music, and the discovery by some jazz critics that certain Serious musicians sustain themselves rhythmically better than others has led them to suggest that these musicians swing. It must be plain, however, that such swinging, if it can be so called, is tame when compared with the jazz musician's flight. It is probably not too much to say that, from the jazz musician's point of view, much Serious music, and especially music written or influenced by the German symphonists, however admirable, can seem to be comparatively earthbound.

The dramatic, reflective and recitative character of nineteenth-century Serious music exacted a price in rhythmic debility, and the cost is conspicuous in most contemporary Serious music, especially in the dodecaphonic, which often seems incapable of any movement or rhythmic buoyancy at all. The dynamic faculty of tempo changes, both sudden and gradual, and all the dramatic inflection inherent in various types of acceleration and retardation, while they served an "interpretive" or "expressive" purpose in European music, also contributed to the weakening of the beat as a phenomenon collectively anticipated and collectively experienced.

This may most easily and properly be appreciated by comparing familiar compositions in their appropriate chronology with an eye to their movement characteristics. Almost any pairing selected at random will do: a Brandenburg concerto and a Strauss tone poem; *The Marriage of Figaro* and *Elektra;* a symphony by Haydn or Mozart and a symphony by Brahms, Bruckner or Mahler; *Fidelio* and *Wozzeck*. Several rhythmic facts are established immediately. The earlier pieces move more easily and more spontaneously. They are less dependent upon an urge to move communicated and regulated by a conductor. The pulsation seems to originate not in the conductor's beat but in the music itself. One has the feeling, with the older music, that an orchestra, given the beat, could carry on without further prodding or guidance, as the jazz band does today. With Bruckner and Mahler, not to speak of Schoenberg and Berg, one feels that the orchestra, without the conductor, would not make much progress.

In other words, during the ultimate phase of European music, where more than a few were gathered together, a conductor was required to determine and sustain the pulse, to make it explicit and to regulate it. The principal dynamic resource was the vertical tension of chords and chord progressions combined with contrasts in the intensity of sound, rather than horizontal or linear tensions of melody supported by pulse. But not even in the eighteenth century, nor in the waltzes, polkas and marches of a later day, did the beat have the propulsive force that it has in jazz today, nor had the musician the same easy, rocking relationship to it.

The harmonic wealth of European music and the variety and efficiency of its instruments, particularly in its later phases, sufficed to disguise or compensate for its rhythmic poverty. Compared with the rhythms of Indian, Southeast Asian, Arabian, African, Chinese or Japanese music, the rhythms of our own Western (European) music have been primitive and rudimentary—a meager assortment of stereotyped patterns in elementary forms of simple and compound time, the pulse so weak, and so abused in the conventions of *interpretive* performance, that in any kind of large ensemble it has had to be articulated by a time beater.

Twentieth-century Serious composers, notably Stravinsky

and Bartók, have been aware of the debility, and they have even looked to rhythm as well as to the possible extensions of tonality—or a breakthrough into atonality—for a way around their harmonic impasse. But instead of going back to a basic meter, they chose to "break the tyranny of the bar line" by constant changes of rhythmic pattern. And in the end they often destroyed what little pulse had survived.

Not that the bar line might not well be broken. It is an artificial device, a convenience in keeping track of melodic rather than rhythmic progress. The composer's revolt was not so much against the bar line as against the regularity of its occurrence. In place of the traditional adherence to consecutive bars, each with the same number of beats, he experimented with a kind of rhythm in which the number of beats to the bar was constantly changed. His purpose was to emphasize the rhythmic character and content of his music by providing rhythmic variety. But the result was merely a superficial sophistication; and it deprived the music of rhythmic intelligibility.

American Popular music, meanwhile, guided by the black jazz musician, found, in the combination of an *explicit* beat and the musician's swinging relationship to the beat, the rhythmic affirmation sought by the Serious composer in an artful manipulation of the beat. No cerebration was involved. It was spontaneous combustion, proceeding from the coincidence of Africa and Europe in the Americas—North, Central and South—with Africa providing the new ingredient. Worldwide acceptance confirmed its contemporary viability— and the end of the European epoch in Western music.

It is not, of course, *just* the explicit beat that sets off jazz from Serious, or European, music. Marches, as well as waltzes, polkas and other dances, have had an *explicit* beat without sounding like jazz. More fundamental and more

decisive is what Gunther Schuller, in his *Early Jazz* (1968),
has termed, ingeniously, the *democratization* of the beat.

"By the 'democratization' of rhythmic values," he writes,
"I mean very simply that in jazz so-called weak beats (or
weak parts of rhythmic units) are *not* underplayed as in
'classical' music. Instead, they are brought up to the level of
strong beats, and very often even emphasized *beyond* the
strong beat. The jazz musician does this not only by maintaining an equality of dynamics among 'weak' and 'strong'
elements, but also by preserving the full sonority of notes,
even though they may happen to fall on weak parts of a
measure. . . . A manifestation of the same principle is the
so-called drum backbeat on the second and fourth beats of
a bar, especially popular in modern jazz drumming and rock
'n' roll music. Similarly, the average jazz musician will count
1-2-3-4 but snap his fingers on 2 and 4, thus putting greater
emphasis on these ordinarily weak beats than on 1 and 3.
(What a far cry from the 'HUT 2-3-4, HUT 2-3-4' of military
marches!) "

This democratization of the beat has a profound effect on
the jazz musician's phrasing. And here again, Schuller, I
think, has managed more successfully than anyone else to
define what it is that distinguishes the jazz from the "classical" phrase:

"In the performance of 'classical' music, for example, there
is a hierarchy of elemental relationships in which pitch is
considered more important than rhythm. . . . The good
'classical' musician will, of course, connect notes so as to produce a phrase; this is a minimum requirement of all music.
But to phrase is not yet to swing; and even a minimal
amount of comparative listening will confirm the fact that
in ordinary 'classical' phrasing the rhythmic impetus is often
relegated to a secondary role. . . .

"For the jazz musician, on the other hand, pitch is unthinkable without a rhythmic impulse at least as strong; rhythm is as much a part of musical expression as pitch or timbre—and possibly more important. This extra dimension in the rhythmic impulse of a jazz phrase is what we call 'swing.' "

Thus, while it is certainly correct to describe the difference between jazz and Serious (between Afro-American and European) as essentially rhythmic, it is essential to comprehend the rhythmic difference. It is not a question of difference in the counting of bars, nor a question of syncopation in the inherited European sense. It is a question of the *explicit* and *democratized* beat as a supporting and sustaining structural force, and of the jazz musician's assiduous exploitation of its propulsive faculties. This, and the related melodic characteristics of attack, contour and cadence, we owe to the black musician. All else in jazz can be related to European models or is colored by European influence. But it is the African contribution that makes all the difference. And it is because this African element is so *different* from any musical element retained in our European heritage that one acknowledges not just a new style, but a new idiom.

Because he perceives the rhythm of jazz both incompletely and imperfectly, the Serious musician tends to regard jazz not only as basically rhythmic but also as rhythmically inferior, bound to the beat and lacking subtlety and refinement. Accustomed to thinking in terms of harmonic rather than rhythmic criteria, and finding nothing harmonically new, he overlooks that musical element in which jazz is more sophisticated than his own music.

The jazz musician, instead of being governed in his melodic progress, as the Serious musician is, by a pattern of beats counted and fractionally subdivided, is free to distribute accents on instants of time undisclosed by any *fractional* sub-

69

division of the bar. His music may be written and felt in a four-to-the-bar pattern, and he may count it accordingly; his melodies may be constructed in orderly eight-bar periods, but the regularity and force of the beat permit and support a freedom of melodic flight denied to his Serious-musician colleague. When the Serious musician deviates rhythmically, he takes the beat with him. When the jazz musician deviates, the beat remains where he left it, an explicit point of reference; and his deviation becomes a source of structural tension. Essential to this rhythmic stability is a rhythm section, normally comprising drums, piano and double bass. Some players and singers can swing without it, the pulse being implied, or provided by the musician's own feet or popping fingers. But most musicians swing more freely, and can build greater rhythmic propulsion and tension, when the pulse is fed by another player.

The Serious-music lover, at this point, may well question the purpose of all that percussive apparatus in a symphony orchestra, and of the numerous hired hands who tend it, if the contribution of the lone jazz drummer, drawing on his arsenal of drums, bongos, tom-toms and cymbals, is so distinctively important. One is tempted to reply that it represents a waste of time and money; for the symphony percussionist is rarely fully employed, and is often enough not employed usefully at all.

A less impertinent and more helpful answer was provided by Harold Farberman, percussionist of the Boston Symphony Orchestra, in the April 1956 issue of *High Fidelity*. "The jazz drummer," he wrote, "plays *within his organization and is at the pulsating heart of it*. Most serious composers, on the other hand, seem to write percussion parts as an afterthought, and, therefore, they generally write for percussion *outside the inner fabric of the music*." (The italics are mine.) In other words, percussion, in European music, unless it is a drum or a cymbal in a marching band, is an adjunct of orchestration, a resource of color and emphasis rather than pulse.

Farberman suggests elsewhere that the American Serious composer, if he really wants to catch the rhythm of American music, "must naturally go to the pulsating source, learn more about percussion, particularly the varied art of the jazz drummers. When he is able to capture the 'swing' of American jazz in his writing for the whole orchestra—including percussion—then the legendary and much joked-about 'American symphony' may finally come to life."

The observations are acute, but the conclusion is dubious. Nobody has yet been able to make a string section swing. Most symphony wind players cannot swing, either, and certainly they cannot swing sectionally. A swinging symphony would also be economic as well as musical nonsense. In order to capture the "swing" of jazz, the Serious composer would have to eliminate most of the symphony orchestra. It would get in his way, just as it has always got in the way of Stan Kenton when he enlarged the jazz band to accommodate a symphonic, or, as he calls it, a "neophonic" sound.

The two idioms are rhythmically incompatible, mutually exclusive, reflecting two essentially different approaches to the achievement and experience of musical communication. The distinctive element is rhythm—the steady pulse, the *explicit* beat, swinging as opposed to arithmetically calculated accentuation. European music, particularly of the thoughtful, dramatic, discursive, graphic kind that flourished in the German-dominated nineteenth century, cannot accept it, any more than jazz can accept the purposefully arbitrary and wayward rhythm of the German symphonists. Bach can usually accommodate a rhythm section, as demonstrated by the Swingle Singers and Jacques Loussier; and so can Handel

71

and Vivaldi; but even with Haydn and Mozart it is felt as an incongruity, and from Beethoven on it is a disaster, an antibody that must be expelled.

This pulse—and the phrasing inspired by the musician's swinging relationship to the pulse—is what distinguishes American from European music; and it is characteristic of every variety of American music, including all but the oldest forms of country-and-western. Remove the swing from New Orleans and Dixieland and you have a marching band. Take it from a swing band and you have a *concerto grosso*. Without it the music of a jazz combo would be Baroque chamber music. Eliminate it from country-and-western and get Anglo-Saxon balladry. Rock 'n' roll, without the beat, will neither rock nor roll. What the jazz musician and the jazz critic think of as jazz is, I believe, simply Afro-American music at its most sophisticated level. It is also the music in which the pulsative, swinging characteristic is the most advanced, the most pronounced and the most conspicuous.

One who shares this view is Friedrich Gulda, the Austrian pianist, who, alone among the top category of Serious virtuosos, has sensed in jazz the only truly contemporary music and has gone on—against much prejudice in both camps—to become a distinguished practitioner. In an exchange of letters with me in 1956, shortly after he had made musical history of a kind by sitting in with the Modern Jazz Quartet at Birdland, following a recital of Beethoven sonatas in Carnegie Hall, Gulda said:

I would agree in principle that indigenous American music must be regarded as an entity. The question of what derives from what, however, is almost unanswerable, since the various trends and directions continually overlap. One thing is certain; namely, that jazz is the best part of American music. With this qualification, one can recognize the totality of American music, distinguishing between good, bad and indifferent in the time-honored manner.

Where jazz begins and ends is anybody's guess—or opinion. It's like asking where *good* begins, or *bad.* Jazz, as a term, is as obsolete as Serious, Classical, Popular and all the rest. Better for everyone had it been buried with King Oliver, leaving musicians to be musicians, free of categorical and prejudicial labels. What matters is that the drumbeat and the rhythmic tensions and the hortatory ecstasy of African music have entered the bloodstream of Western music—and Western music will never be the same again!

"A Performer's Art"

IN IDENTIFYING a variety of misconceptions and superstitions about the distinctive elements and characteristics of Afro-American music, I have slighted, purposefully, the familiar contention that jazz is "a performer's art." This is the gambit offered most frequently and confidently by those who know that all the talk of syncopation, improvisation, illiteracy and flatted thirds and sevenths is either nonsense or irrelevant. I have slighted it thus far because it is neither a misconception nor a superstition. It is the truth.

And the pejorative insinuation that "a performer's art" differs from, and is intrinsically inferior to, "a composer's art" or "an interpreter's art" is, in my view, abominable. It is also instructive; for the implicit acquiescence in the separation of composition and performance goes a long way toward explaining the separation of composer and audience that precipitated the decline, and now documents the fall, of Western music in its European phase. It helps us to understand why, for the past hundred years or more, Serious music has grown steadily less musical.

Time was, in European music—and it was a better time—

when composer and performer were more often united in the same person, as exemplified in the careers and in the compositions of Handel, Bach, Corelli, Vivaldi, Scarlatti, Mozart, Beethoven, Hummel, Clementi, Spohr, Weber, Moscheles, Liszt, Chopin, Mendelssohn, Paganini, Brahms, Vieuxtemps, Wieniawski, Rubinstein, Sarasate, Bruckner, and Rachman-inoff. There have always been, to be sure, composers who were not especially celebrated as virtuoso instrumentalists—Gluck, Haydn, Schubert, Schumann, Berlioz, Verdi, Wagner, Tchaikovsky, Strauss and Mahler—but they were all immediately concerned with performance, either in the theater or in the concert hall; and Berlioz, Wagner, Strauss and Mahler were all among the greatest conductors of their time.

Because what the European composer-performers wrote has survived all memory of how, and even of what, they played, and because some of the masters were not memorable performers, the Serious-music community, little by little, has come to think of music as something to be read or memorized, of the composer as essentially a writer, and of composition as a separate and superior calling.

Although improvisation is, inescapably, composition, it is not thought of as composition, or even as music, in any worthy sense. The jazz musician is denied the dignity accorded the composer because not everything that he composes is first written down, or, necessarily, written down afterward, or, once written down, considered immutable. And he is denied the dignity accorded the Serious-music performer because the latter is an "interpreter" of presumably great music.

The musician, in other words, who makes up his music as he goes along, or makes up a good deal of it, or who rarely plays the same music twice in the same way, is, we are given to understand, inferior to the musician who makes no music of his own. For all his undisputed virtuosity and inventive fancy, the jazz musician cannot, we are led to believe, be granted equality with the Serious musician who can read and play the notes written down for him by Bach, Mozart, Beethoven, Brahms and Wagner a century or so ago.

"As I see it," André Previn told Miles Kington, jazz critic of the London *Times,* in the fall of 1967, "the basic difference between classical music and jazz is that in the former the music is always greater than its performance—Beethoven's Violin Concerto, for instance, is always better than any possible performance of it—whereas the way jazz is performed is always more important than what is being played; and as I am more interested in the music than its performance, this partly explains why I have left jazz. But this is quite personal. You can't really compare the two; saying that Brahms's First is better than Charlie Parker is like saying that this lamp is better than that window."

What Previn is really saying, I think, is that, as between Brahms and Parker, he prefers Brahms, certainly an unobjectionable preference, and that classical music interests him more than jazz, which is all right, too. But his insistence that in classical music the music is always better than its performance implies a severe restriction of what is admissible as classical music. It may be argued that no performance has ever fully encompassed and projected the substance of Beethoven's Violin Concerto, but I would be very surprised to hear Previn deny that many performers have made much classical music sound better than it actually is; in other words, that in classical music, too, the *way* may be more important than the *what.*

But he would probably argue that even the best Serious performer, playing the worst classical music, is still playing only what the composer has written, and that what he plays is *the music,* whereas in jazz even the best composition may be treated only as a point of departure for the performer, good or bad. To take it amiss, however, that a performer's contribution might be more important than a composer's reflects, in my opinion, a nineteenth-century German view of the distinction between composer and performer, and a nineteenth-century German notion, too, of what music is all about.

This view may be persuasive if one has to do with a Beethoven or a Brahms. But their like has not been around for a long time. What matters is, after all, what one hears, whether the source is Brahms or Parker or the Beatles. Previn's statement that, in jazz, "the way it is performed is almost always more important than what is being played" ignores the fact that the jazz musician's *way* is also his *what.* It may be largely his own; but does that make it inferior, necessarily, not to Beethoven or Brahms but to Stockhausen, Cage or Boulez?

Such inverted thinking is, of course, a consequence of the composer idolatry inherited from a time in the cycle of European music when composers were, indeed, the great creative artists—and, often enough, the greatest performers, too. It also proceeds from a failure to submit the conventions of evaluation to periodic review in the light of new circumstances. While it is hardly conceivable that a sensible critic today would claim for any contemporary composer the genius of a Bach, a Haydn, a Mozart, a Beethoven, a Schubert, a Verdi or a Wagner, the great art implicit and explicit in what those composers wrote has left a legacy of sanctity to the written notes and to the man who now writes them. This legacy has survived several decades of relatively undistinguished and all too often unintelligible composition.

The performer, at the same time—and I am speaking now of the Serious musician rather than the jazz musician—has been increasingly discouraged and frustrated as a creative artist. In the time when the music that now comprises the standard repertoire was new, the performer enjoyed a considerable latitude, either as himself the composer or as one whom the composer welcomed as collaborator and colleague, the more so since almost every great performer, singers excepted, was also a composer. Deprived now of a contemporary music congenial to himself and his public, the performer-interpreter has had to concentrate largely on old music, devoting himself to a repertoire so familiar to his listeners, and so revered by them, that any significant departure from what have become the conventions of interpretation and performance will be denounced as sacrilege.

The performer in Serious music, including the almighty conductor, is expected to play the notes, all the notes and nothing but the notes; and he is expected to play them exactly as written. Critics and many lay listeners follow his performance in the concert hall or on the phonograph record in the living room, score in hand, holding him accountable for every dot and double dot, for every eighth and quarter rest, for every expression mark, for every indication of tempo and dynamics, for every retard and every acceleration, for every crescendo, diminuendo and *fermata*. That some performers still achieve distinction despite the appallingly narrow range of options speaks for their ingenuity, as does their proud rationalization of this pedantry as "fidelity to the score."

It must seem inevitable, however, that any musician constantly subject to such inhibitions and restraints will be—or become—emotionally and imaginatively handicapped and stunted. He has no music of his own, nor can he play anyone else's music with the immediacy that it had for those to whom it was originally addressed, or expect from his listeners the same immediate response. He must be temporally neutral. Certain interpretive options remain, but they are options of refinement and degree, and even these are governed by a contemporary public's notions of how old music should be updated—or be made to conform to contemporary taste—without patent violation of scripture.

Given such constraints as these, compounded by the stagnation of the repertoire, it is a tribute to the Serious musician's skills, diligence and patience, sometimes even to his intelligence, that he is not a duller fellow than he is, especially the orchestra musician, playing more or less the same notes in more or less the same way under the daily supervision of a variety of opinionated conductors year in and year out, or the itinerant virtuoso, condemned for the rest of his life to a small bag of viable concertos by Mozart, Beethoven and Brahms.

Less admirable, except for the ingenuity of the convolution, is the manner in which this kind of sterile musicianship is represented as superior to that of the jazz musician, playing his own admittedly excellent music in his own admittedly excellent way for his own admittedly sophisticated audience. In a breathtaking feat of intellectual prestidigitation, artistic virtue is suddenly seen as debility, and debility as virtue, even when the jazz musician's virtues are demonstrably identical with what is still counted as virtue in the early masters of European music: invention, originality, the ability to sublimate a contemporary Popular music, a virtuosity that led to the improvement of musical instruments and the introduction and development of new ones, in vocal music a comprehension and appreciation of a lively vernacular, and, in retrospect, the faculty of speaking musically for one's own time.

The jazz musician's invention, for example, is held against him because he keeps on inventing; today's invention may supersede yesterday's and fail to survive tomorrow's. The listener, of course, is always hearing something more or less fresh and new, and he may enjoy the invention and the novelty. But the source of his enjoyment cannot be Art, since what he hears is of the moment and for the moment. And Art is presumed to be eternal.

Over a longer period of time, the jazz musician's invention may change fundamentally, responding to generation-to-generation—even season-to-season—fluctuations in public taste; and this, in the conventional view, is very bad, betraying an unfashionable concern for the listener's pleasure and a readiness to adapt one's music to the listener's expectations. In order to be an Artist, according to the canons of the Serious-music community, the musician must play Baroque music authentically and nineteenth-century music in a manner tailored to the tastes and expectations of the twentieth century.

The habit—common to Serious musicians and Serious critics—of disparaging the music of the jazz musician as impermanent and non-enduring is, if anything, more presumptuous than their dismissal of it as "a performer's art." Whether the jazz musician's music is "enduring" or not remains to be seen. The probability is that some of it will endure and most of it will not, which would duplicate the endurance characteristics of most Serious music of every period.

Aiming for durability would, in any case, seem to be putting the cart before the horse. A more sober procedure would be to accept mortality and to address oneself to a mortal audience here and now. Evidence of life, certainly, as documented in a living audience's pleasure, must be viewed as a first step toward even a qualified immortality.

"Yes, it may be good, but will it last?" is a cliché of the more sophisticated Serious musician's commentary on jazz. To which I reply: Who cares? What does it matter? Let the future look out for itself. What matters is how the music of our own time speaks to us and for us. And let us hope that each future age will have a music of its own, for its own sake and especially for the sake of the future musician, and that it will be more perceptive than our own age has been in recognizing its own music. Durability may be accepted as evidence of quality in any music; but it is not the objective, and it is not necessarily desirable. No more terrible burden for the creative musician can be imagined than an established repertoire. It crowds him out.

It is just this accumulation of a "standard" repertoire of surviving masterpieces, and the Serious musician's dependence upon it for his own survival, that has focused attention upon the composer rather than the performer as the supreme musician, and upon a written record in the form of a full score as indispensable to substantial composition. Which seems odd when one remembers that Serious music counts among its masterpieces compositions of the seventeenth century containing nothing more than a melody line and an unfigured bass.

But ever since Beethoven furrowed his brow and shook his fist at the heavens, composition has been reckoned too solemn a matter to be left to a performer's discretion or to accommodate a performer's elaboration. Earlier composers rejoiced in a less somber disposition; furthermore, they did not look upon improvisation as trivial. What we read now about the *ex tempore* accomplishments of Bach, Mozart, Beethoven, Chopin and Liszt should make us hesitant to assume any limits to improvisational inspiration. And the music of the best jazz musicians proves that the improvisational faculty has not been lost to our human kind. The phonograph record, moreover, is far superior as a preservative to any system ever devised for *writing* music.

Overlooked is the jazz musician's independence of scrip-

ture as evidence of an indigenous style and of stylistic security. What he plays is *his* music, in a collective and social
sense, and nobody else's, and he need not worry about how
somebody played it, or may have played it, a hundred or two
hundred years ago. He can do with it what he pleases, governed in his fancy only by conventions or by the impulse to
depart from convention. If he is playing another's music, he
will know instinctively and exactly when he must be literal
to safeguard the ensemble and when he is expected to contribute something of his own by deviation or improvisation.
And he will know, in terms of what is stylistically permissible, precisely what to add, and how.

Music and style, in his world, are one and the same thing.
The style is the music, and music the style, as was true of the
older eras of European music. Manfred F. Bukofzer has made
a point of this in the Preface to his *Music in the Baroque Era*
(1947). "It is a strange though incontestable fact," he writes,
"that by far the great majority of music books deal with
composers rather than their music. This attitude is a survival
of the hero-worship that characterizes the nineteenth-century
approach to music as well as the other arts. In a history of a
single musical period the shortcomings of such an approach
become particularly obvious. A musical era receives its inner
unity from the musical style and can be historically understood only in terms of stylistic development."

So it is with jazz; and it is this identification with style, and
the acceptance of stylistic discipline, that distinguish jazz
improvisation from the aleatoric or "chance" *ex tempore*
procedures of some avant-garde Serious music. When a jazz
instrumentalist improvises, it is a sense of style that dictates
his choice of notes and their rhythmic ordering. When a
Popular singer deviates from the melody as written, or from
the indicated time values of the notes, he will be guided by

his own sense of what is appropriate both to the music and to the occasion. The pianist extemporizing from the chords, the bass player filling in a bass line, and the drummer lifting and driving will all be responding to stylistic requirements commonly felt and commonly understood.

In this respect, style is more important than composition, or, to put it boldly, style is the supreme composer, providing the esthetic frame of reference and the basic communicative conventions from which each individual musician works. It is the evolution and acceptance of a style, and the accomplishments of the executant musician within that style, rather than the theories and practice of any single individual, that mirror the lyrical predilections of a society or a generation. Forceful and imaginative individuals, like Beethoven and Wagner, can expand and extend a style. They can challenge its conventions. But the style and its conventions are a prerequisite for their work; and its claim to validity can be sustained only by the verdict of a contemporary audience. It is precisely the want of a contemporary style congenial to musician and listener alike that has confirmed the sterility of the European idiom in the twentieth century.

The debacle was a long time in the making. There had been a common style in the eighteenth century and earlier. Even the greatest composers accepted its conventions, and all but the very greatest and most familiar of their compositions may well be difficult to identify and distinguish from the best music of their contemporaries. Some composers were better than others, but they were not conspicuously different. Beethoven, probably, was the first to disclose a unique physiognomy; and from his time on, there was an ever-increasing emphasis on idiosyncratic originality.

The result was not one common style but many styles. Each composer had to develop his own stock-in-trade, his own readily identifiable manner, and particularly his own harmonic manner, with a consequent acceleration of the raid on the not inexhaustible resources of chromatic harmony. Anything he did that reminded the listener of what anybody else had done was promptly chalked up against him as "reminiscent" or "imitative" by vigilant Beckmessers. A century earlier, Bach and Handel could plagiarize themselves and others without fear of criticism. The new nineteenth-century composer-hero was haunted by what Wyndham Lewis so aptly called "the demon of progress in modern art."

Bartók and Prokofiev were the last who could still make something both original and stylistically convincing from the debris of the European idiom. Stravinsky, Schoenberg and even Berg could achieve vitality in their earlier works, for all three had talent, and there was yet a shred of traditional resources left. But Schoenberg's gamble on an adventurous and brainy theory reckoned without the immutability of human musical instinct, ignoring the implications of the cadences of speech and the insistent pulse of the human body. And Stravinsky, looking for sustenance in a tidy neoclassicism spiced with fashionable dissonance, fell afoul of his own cleverness and has been floundering ever since, including a discreditable pass at serialism.

Popular recognition and acceptance of a common style by a large general public would seem to be a precondition for any general musical prosperity. The conventional history of European music is deceptive in its concentration upon those few composers whose finest accomplishments stand out so conspicuously from their contemporaries that we tend to forget how many excellent contemporaries they had, and how much all the music of any flourishing period had in common. It is customary, for example, to speak of Mozart's *style,* or of Bach's *style,* or of Haydn's, when it would be more accurate to speak of individual characteristics within a common style.

It was the easy and unconstrained access to a common style that made it possible, in the seventeenth and eighteenth centuries, for most performers to be composers and for most composers to be performers. The latter, conversant with the conventions of composition and responsive to contemporary taste and expectations, could alter, add to, or subtract from the written notes without any consciousness of stylistic hazard; and the composer would anticipate this collaboration by leaving a good deal to the performer's discretion, just as a jazz composition or arrangement today leaves more or less extensive areas to be filled in by the individual performer.

It was the very masterpieces of European music, paradoxically, which led to the disintegration of a European style. Where earlier composers had accepted the discipline of stylistic conventions as a challenge to ingenuity and artisanship, Beethoven, Chopin, Berlioz, Liszt, Wagner, Verdi and Debussy challenged any discipline but their own. In their music one recognizes distinctively personal styles rather than mere individual idiosyncracies within a common style. The defiance was applauded, and the composer seemed vindicated in his assertion of autonomy.

We know now that the structural resources available within the traditional frame of reference of European music could not forever yield an infinity of individual styles; nor could composers long support the requirement of continuous and unblemished originality. The composer had always to be on guard not only against imitating other composers, dead or alive, but also against imitating himself. Because some few composers had been geniuses, and inferior composers had been forgotten, it was assumed that composer and genius were somehow synonymous, and nothing less than genius was now expected of anyone who felt called to be a composer.

The expectation may have been flattering, and the status associated with it welcome, but failure to fill the bill brought frustration, disappointment and ruin. And no longer could the former easy collaboration between composer and performer be sustained. The composer's individuality was not only sacrosanct; it was essential to his deity. He, alone, was assumed to be master of his own tongue, and his scores became ever more explicit and ever more restrictive in their instructions to the performer. But now, speaking a language of his own, with whom could he speak? And how?

In jazz, the relationship between composer and performer, and between musician and audience, has always been based, until recently, on the mutual acceptance of a common language. It differs not at all from comparable relationships in European music in the seventeenth and eighteenth centuries. There is even the almost axiomatic union of composer and performer in the same person. The jazz musician has had to accept, of course, the discipline of a style, just as Haydn and Mozart did; but within this style he has enjoyed greater freedom than the Serious composer enjoys today, the latter condemned to the search for a style of his own, or to the acceptance of dogma imposed by other composers.

And he has enjoyed greater freedom, of course, as well as greater responsibility, than the Serious performer-interpreter, restricted to the repetition of what somebody else has written. What the jazz musician plays is his own music, in a collective sense, allowing him to speak for himself in a language shared with his fellows. Working within a common style, he is stylistically secure, not in the safe haven of a score and the explicit instruction but in the open spaces of musical adventure and invention, where, with style as his guide and companion, he can move freely without fear of going astray.

The more knowledgeable and objective among Serious musicians and Serious-music critics may recognize the basic similarity between the role of the jazz performer and the performance practices of older eras of European music; but they cannot reconcile the conventions of jazz with the later conventions of European music, closer to their own musical experience and expectations. Theirs is, as a rule, a progressive view of musical history. Instinctively, or by rationalization, they feel that music has come a long way since the seventeenth and eighteenth centuries—and a long way from the intimate give-and-take of performer and listener—and they feel, too, that while it may have been all well and good for the performer to be the center of attention two and three hundred years ago, and to be granted the privilege of interpretive and creative discretion, it is not all well and good now, with the masterpieces of the nineteenth century to remind us how much more important the composer can be than any mere performer.

One is tempted to suggest that the validity of such a view depends upon the composer and the quality of his composition, but this would seem to be suggesting, in turn, that any music's capacity to accommodate, or benefit from, the creative participation of the performer is in inverse ratio to its quality as composition. And we know that a performer's creative or elaborative participation in European music in the seventeenth and eighteenth centuries was not thought to be a reflection upon the work of the composer. It was just as likely to be thought a compliment.

The art of the jazz musician has something in common, it seems to me, with that of a Maria Callas, who, in reviving forgotten operas by Cherubini, Rossini, Donizetti and Bellini, was not so much turning lesser metals into gold as simply disclosing how much gold was always there, awaiting the singer who would know how it must be mined. Here, too, was music conceived in anticipation of a great performer's contribution—a Pasta, a Rubini, a Persiani, a Colbran, or a

Lablache. And this, in turn, was a perpetuation of the older Italian tradition of composer-performer collaboration. The essential conventions and traditions of Italian opera succumbed to German fashion in the course of the nineteenth century, and so did the music. It seemed dated and bare until Callas came along, not because it was bad but because the essential style of performance had been lost, anathematized by Schumann, Wagner and Bülow as incompatible with the aspirations of enlightened German romanticism and hostile to the German view of a composer's prerogatives.

One can imagine an analogous situation a hundred and fifty years from now, assuming that the phonograph had never been invented, if musicians of 2120 were exposed to compositions by Duke Ellington, or to songs that owe the special enchantment they have for us to the art of Sinatra and Fitzgerald. They would be in the position of those who, today, try to reconstruct the art of a Bach, a Scarlatti or a Buxtehude from the notes they left behind, or who would like to sing as Farinelli and Caffarelli sang.

There may have been something to say for the more explicit notation of the nineteenth-century composer, and for his tendency to look to the tractable instrument of the orchestra rather than to the ephemeral art of the solo performer as the custodian of his gospel, however much the performer's art was thus circumscribed. The composer's procedures reduced the hazard of stylistic deviation by performers of succeeding generations in the days before phonograph and tape recording assured a more reliable source of reference. But it also tended to reduce the performer to the role of intermediary between the absent composer and the very present audience, to deprive music of all the charm of spontaneous elaboration and decoration, and to extinguish the eternal magic of the virtuoso singer or instrumentalist out there in front of a listening public with something of his own to say in the listener's own language—and both the privilege and the responsibility of saying it.

"The progress of musical art," says Joseph Machlis, Professor of Music, Queens College of the City of New York, in his *The Enjoyment of Music, An Introduction to Perceptive Listening* (1955), "demanded the victory over improvisation. The composer ultimately established his right to choose the notes, the performer being limited to playing or, at most, interpreting them."

This formulation concedes to an institution known as "the composer" a God-given monopoly as the source of music and as the arbiter of its dispensation; and it seems to assume that the composer's victory over improvisation was in the public interest. It would have been an unexceptionable formulation at the close of the nineteenth century, and it represents an orthodox view to this day.

Reassessment in the light of the experience of our own century, however, might turn victory into catastrophe and victors into hapless victims. The composer, in subduing the performer, reduced to serfdom an indispensable ally, depriving himself of that intimacy with an audience which is the performer's privilege and without which all music-making is vain. The art of the jazz musician, at the same time, has revived the composer-performer identity that was once the glory of Western music.

Those of the Serious-music community who speak disparagingly of "a performer's art," implying a categorical and generic inferiority to the art and responsibility of the composer or to the accomplishment of the Serious-music performer-interpreter, forget, or have never known, how much the performer's art may also be composition, whether written down or not, and how wonderful that art can be.

The world of Serious music is the poorer for it.

89

The
Afro-American Epoch

THE HISTORY of Western music conventionally identifies a succession of more or less cleanly circumscribed epochs, *e.g.,* Medieval, Renaissance, Baroque, Rococo, Classic, Romantic and Modern, the last of these dating from about 1910 and continuing into the present.

These terms, satisfactory as they may be as symbols of stylistic and conceptual phenomena, give no hint of the succession of national and cultural dominions associated with each major epoch. The Renaissance, for instance, was dominated by the Netherlands, the Baroque by Italy, the Classic by Austria-Bohemia and the Romantic by Germany. And it is this phenomenon, historically noted and fully documented but critically slighted, that may provide, in my opinion, a clue to a better understanding of what has happened, and is still happening, in our own century.

If we look for a corresponding national dominion—and a continuity of the pattern of successive national or cultural dominions—we can find persuasive evidence that we are now in the midst of what future musical historians may well designate the Afro-American epoch. The analogies are ob-

vious, the discrepancies inconsequential and easily rationalized, the differences profound but not irreconcilable. In
each case, or epoch, we have the music and the musicians of a
single nation or culture proving to be so irresistibly attractive
to other nations and other cultures as to determine the
musical physiognomy of an entire civilization or age.

Paul Henry Lang's *Music in Western Civilization* (1941)
includes full-page maps showing (1) the distribution of
Flemish (Netherlands) composers throughout Europe between 1470 and 1550; (2) the distribution of Italian composers throughout Europe and the New World between 1675
and 1750; and (3) the distribution of Austro-Bohemian
composers throughout Europe and North America between
1700 and 1775, the chronological overlap reflecting the period of transition from the Baroque to the Classic epoch.
Lang could have, and should have, added a fourth map, dated
a century later, showing a similar dispersal of German composers, performers and teachers throughout the same area,
with a heavy concentration in the United States.

A corresponding map, drawn today and showing the dispersal of American music, would have fewer American musicians in residence abroad, but it would reflect a similar
saturation and an even more pervasive universality. It would
also cover a far greater area: the larger part, in fact, of the
terrestrial globe. The discrepancy as to residence abroad is
purely technical. Where music was once propagated locally
by the individual, it is now propagated generally and instantly by the phonograph record, the radio and the motion-
picture sound track, supported and stimulated by the jet-
borne itinerant musician.

Many American jazz musicians have established residence
in foreign lands for longer or shorter periods, including particularly black musicians who have found foreign soil more

hospitable than their own—Sidney Bechet, Bill Coleman, Don Byas, Albert Nicholas, Don Redman, Buck Clayton, Johnny Griffin and many more—but theirs has been an auxiliary influence. The same is true of the scores of foreign jazz musicians who have emigrated to the United States, or who have come as visitors for extended periods.

The primary influence was, initially, the phonograph record, which, as far back as the late 1920s and early 1930s, made it possible for thousands of Europeans to become jazz enthusiasts who had never heard a first-class jazz musician in person. Only the phonograph record can account for the astonishing circumstance that Europeans, including the British, were well ahead of Americans in assessing correctly the genius of the first great jazz musicians, notably Bechet, Louis Armstrong and Duke Ellington, and in distinguishing the idiomatic difference between jazz and a Popular music derived from traditional European models.

It was Constant Lambert, an Englishman, who, in *Music Ho!* (1934), could say of Duke Ellington:

The real interest of Ellington's records lies not so much in their color, brilliant though it may be, as in the amazingly skillful proportions in which the color is used. I do not only mean skillful as compared with other jazz composers, but as compared with so-called highbrow composers. I know of nothing in Ravel so dexterous in treatment as the varied solos in the middle of the ebullient "Hot and Bothered," and nothing in Stravinsky more dynamic than the final section. The combination of themes at this moment is one of the most ingenious pieces of writing in modern music.

Ernest Ansermet, conductor of the Orchestre de la Suisse Romande, had reacted immediately and enthusiastically when he heard Bechet in 1919; and during the 1920s and early 1930s Stravinsky, Milhaud, Ravel, Křenek and others documented their perception in their own compositions. Their failure to understand, or their reluctance to concede, its true significance has been discussed elsewhere. It seems reasonable to suggest, however, that the brevity of their preoccupation reflected an instinctive awareness that more was involved than merely an exotic popular fad; far more, indeed, than could be accommodated within their own traditional European frame of esthetic reference.

Nor can one be certain just what it was that they heard. They may, like Ansermet and Lambert, have heard the real thing. But jazz had already fathered an indigenous Popular music whose immediate international acceptance led to the designation of the 1920s as "the jazz age," and it seems more likely that they were reacting to the bands of Paul Whiteman, Vincent Lopez, Guy Lombardo and Fred Waring, or one of their innumerable European imitators, making foxtrots of the songs of Irving Berlin, Jerome Kern, Vincent Youmans, Cole Porter and George Gershwin, or to the brash and uninhibited vocalism of Al Jolson, Ruth Etting, Ethel Merman, Rudy Vallee and Harry Richman.

None of this music sounds much like what we think of as jazz when we hear it on phonograph records today; but it was, at the time, startlingly and delightfully different from any previous kind of Popular music, and its worldwide appeal may be seen, in retrospect, as demonstrating the timeliness and the inevitability of a radical departure from traditional European musical convention. Something closer to what is now accepted as jazz enjoyed a comparable international acceptance in the succeeding "swing era," as represented in the bands of Benny Goodman, the Dorsey brothers, Glenn Miller and Artie Shaw.

All of this was symptomatic of the debility of the European

musical idioms in Popular music as well as in the more pretentious forms. But few in Europe, and fewer, probably, in America, perceived behind the Popular façade the elements of a great musical art, if only because, at that time, very few were aware of, or had ever heard, the greatest jazz musicians, most of them Negroes. There were "hot clubs," to be sure, and jazz magazines and record collectors, but the enthusiasts of true jazz could be numbered in the low thousands. The effective breakthrough from cult to culture, in the broadest sense of the term, came with the LP record and with the presence, in Europe, North Africa, Japan and Australia, during and after World War II, of millions of American soldiers and civilians.

With the latter and, subsequently, their families, came the Armed Forces Radio Network. The indigenous broadcasting institutions soon discovered the appetite of their own listening public for the music—jazz and Popular—addressed to the occupiers; and they responded promptly with jazz programs of their own, drawing upon the early European connoisseurs for enlightened guidance. These programs were more sophisticated and severe than the American programs, reflecting the European predilection for a more intellectual approach to music. The European treatment of American music on the radio and in television is to this day generally superior, in selection and in the quality of the commentary, to corresponding programs in the United States.

This evidence of an enormous foreign following did not pass unnoticed by those who earn their daily bread by playing for it, and it led to the tours by American jazz musicians that got under way—and not only in Europe—in the 1950s. The enthusiastic—often riotous—welcome accorded the tours of Norman Granz's Jazz at the Philharmonic and the concerts given by the bands of Duke Ellington, Louis Armstrong,

Count Basie, Harry James and Lionel Hampton needs no elaboration. It is now acknowledged as a unique episode of musical history.

And it went farther than that. The 1950s were, it will be remembered, the decade of the Cold War. Very early in this decade, newspaper correspondents and other travelers, returning from tours behind the Iron Curtain, brought back accounts of "black listening," of young musicians in the Communist countries writing down arrangements from radio broadcasts and trying them out in clandestine sessions in cellars, even in cemeteries, of a lively black market in jazz records, and so on.

This all pointed to a disconcerting ambiguity in the representation of the American image abroad. The United States, for the first time in its history, was engaging officially in cultural propaganda; but those to whom this propaganda was entrusted worked from a traditional European concept of culture and from a European assessment of cultural values centered upon European accomplishments, assuming, apparently, that our purpose was to prove ourselves as good Europeans as any. At the same time, a far more representative—and certainly far less European—America, as reflected in its own music, its own motion pictures, its own theater, its own literature and its own individual citizens, was finding a larger and more receptive public without official sponsorship of any kind.

The divergence of a controlled and an uncontrolled projection had been obvious for some years, but until the prospect of political exploitation became apparent there was little disposition in official quarters to question the assumption, as far as music was concerned, that the Philadelphia, Boston and New York orchestras, playing Beethoven and Brahms with a dutiful leavening of Copland, Sessions and Barber, were preferable to jazz as a reflection of American culture. The tendency was rather to intensify the subsidization of our accomplishments in essentially European disciplines as a counterweight to what required no official assistance. The welcome accorded to our great jazz musicians was studiously, even defiantly, ignored by our own diplomatic missions.

Now, suddenly, on Sunday, November 6, 1955, there appeared on the front page of the *The New York Times* a startling three-column headline: UNITED STATES HAS SECRET SONIC WEAPON—JAZZ! The story, by Felix Belair, was datelined Geneva, where Belair, who had no connection with music, was covering a conference of Foreign Ministers. What he wrote was based on what he had heard from fellow correspondents, speaking from firsthand experience, about the clandestine dissemination of jazz in the Communist countries of eastern Europe. Belair was so impressed by what they told him that he retired, that Saturday afternoon, to his room in the Hotel du Rhône, wrote it all out and put it on the wire. His editors in New York, to Belair's amazement, played it on the front page.

There were immediate inquiries at the State Department as to whether any official use were being made of this new weapon, and the State Department, thanks to the foresight of "Chip" Bohlen, then our Ambassador to the Soviet Union, was able to respond with something better than just a blank and aggrieved look. On January 1, 1955, the Voice of America, acting on Ambassador Bohlen's suggestion, had inaugurated a music program planned, written and narrated by a young former disc jockey named Willis Conover. Due partly to Congressional reservations about broadcasting what some legislators thought might emphasize the seamier side of American culture, the program had been beamed initially only to jazz-loving and friendly Scandinavia. The response had been beyond every expectation.

With the stimulus of the *New York Times* spread, the program was increased to one and a half hours a day, six days a week, and given worldwide dissemination. Known as *Music USA,* Conover's programs covered the best of both Popular music and jazz. They were presented—and are still presented —exclusively in English, without a word of political propaganda. Four years later, *The New York Times* again, but now in the Sunday *Magazine,* could print over an article by John S. Wilson: WHO IS CONOVER? ONLY WE ASK.

Conover had, in fact, become one of the most famous of all Americans—everywhere except in America. His listening audience has been estimated at thirty millions a night. His *News Letter* is mailed to 1,300 fan clubs all over the world twice every month. In more recent years, following up his voice with personal visits to his listeners, he has been welcomed everywhere as an ambassador of good will and doer of good deeds—including the Soviet Union and the Communist countries of eastern Europe.

The Voice of America and Willis Conover, after 1955, were no longer alone. America's indigenous music had long been acknowledged as its most original and distinctive contribution to Western culture even by those who occupied the most prestigious and influential positions in the cultural community. But there was—and is still—a persistent reluctance to draw the obvious conclusions and grant it the respectability enjoyed as a matter of course by less vigorous accomplishments more closely attuned to European precedent and tradition. Not even the prospect of political profit could correct or remove the bias; but confronted with facts—demonstrable and politically exploitable—the recalcitrants had to act.

Arrangements were made for sponsored tours by such outstanding musicians and their groups as Louis Armstrong, Count Basie, Duke Ellington, Lionel Hampton, Benny Goodman, Dizzy Gillespie, the Modern Jazz Quartet, Fatha Hines, Dave Brubeck and many more. The program has been on the whole sensibly, if not always knowledgeably, executed, with special attention given to those areas, notably in Asia and Africa, where the prospects of financial profit were insufficient to invite unsubsidized travel.

What makes this history pertinent to an examination of the evolutionary forces at work in music in our century is that the government was reacting—and had to react—to the facts of contemporary musical life. Universal acceptance of jazz as the musical vernacular of youth throughout most of the world was not an accomplishment of official propaganda. The appetite, the acceptance and even a considerable sophistication were already there.

Official and assiduous propagation of America's Serious composers, conversely, had failed to arouse any enthusiasm. And while Europeans usually acknowledged the technical finish of the American orchestras, and the disciplined dexterity of the instrumental virtuosos who accompanied them, they often argued that American efficiency had been achieved at a cost of European sensibility. America's indigenous music, on the other hand, needed no propaganda. It was propaganda that needed the music.

Its dissemination could not, in fact, be stopped, as the Soviets and the Communist nations of eastern Europe had to learn. They felt more acutely than the Western democracies the attraction that this music had for their young. It may have been regarded, in the democracies, as a threat to social and esthetic conventions. The older generation, certainly, heard in it a defiance that defied argument. But in the Communist countries it was seen as a threat to government, since government modestly presumed to determine and regulate taste. Repression was tried, without success, and then various combinations of acquiescence and control. Today there are jazz musicians, jazz clubs and jazz festivals in every country in eastern Europe, including the Soviet Union, and American jazz musicians are frequent and welcome visitors.

What had been overlooked by the cultural propagandists was the new complexion, the new outlook, the new aspirations, the new sense of identity, of the younger intellectuals, who, everywhere and not only in Europe, found in the new indigenous American music an expression of their own break with traditional cultural and social conventions. These young people were readier than their elders, and better able, to appreciate its creative imagination and communicative immediacy. And they were not to be put off by its seeming incompatibility with what had hitherto been accepted universally as immutable criteria of good music. In fact, the innocent ignorance and gay defiance of European tradition added considerably to its lure, just as it also exacerbated the hostility of the older generation.

None of this sense of conflict, of incompatibility, with European conventions has been conspicuous in America's other cultural exports. What America produced in the theater, in literature and in the graphic arts may have disclosed distinctively American characteristics; but there was no radical departure from European precedent and European criteria. But jazz made its own rules and went its own way, responsive only to its own enormous—and youthful—public.

Here, for the first time, was an art for which the older European intellectual could claim no authorship, with which he had no sense of identity, and over which he could exercise no control. He could talk about it, but without the assurance of knowing what he was talking about. He could disparage it as a popular aberration, and this was his habitual tactic, but his intelligence—and the example of his intelligent juniors—told him that there was more to its popularity than just childish delight in a childish fad. His intelligence told him that his musical tradition was in jeopardy.

Those stylistic phenomena in which we recognize the distinguishing characteristics of an epoch, or era, represent, almost by definition, a break with tradition, or at least a departure from convention. But such breaks and departures have rarely been so radical as to destroy or frustrate a sense of cultural continuity, or to suggest an entirely new idiom. In music, the boundaries between one musical epoch and another have been, as a rule, neither finely drawn nor acutely felt. Transition has taken place so gradually, so naturally, so inevitably, and often so nearly imperceptibly, that historians and musicologists are far from unanimous in their conclusions as to just when it began and when it ended.

Beethoven, to be sure, may be felt to represent a radical break with the Classic epoch and to herald very dramatically the new Romantic era. Certainly he created a stir in his own time. But few would contend that even his most adventurous music was not rooted in the music of his immediate predecessors, or that there was not, in the music of Haydn, Mozart and Cherubini, a foretaste of what was to come.

Transition has always excited controversy, of course, some of it heated; but usually it has been the kind of controversy that derives from the familiar tensions of liberal-versus-conservative, progressive-versus-reactionary. Musical language was always changing, and there was resistance to change; but there was no change in the language. The conservative felt that his sense of values was threatened; but cultural continuity was not interrupted, however much it may have been abused. Beethoven's *Missa Solemnis* and Ninth Symphony, his last piano sonatas and even his last quartets could be played by the same musicians who had played Mozart and Haydn. They were heard and applauded by the same audiences, and they were discussed and reviewed, often very perceptively, by the same critics.

Only in the transition from Renaissance to Baroque, in the evolution of tonal, or diatonic, harmony from modal polyphony, had there been previously a break with the past as radical as that which we are experiencing today. The earlier transition from an *ars antiqua* to an *ars nova*, which had ushered in the Renaissance epoch in the early decades of the fourteenth century, had certain similar characteristics, *i.e.*, a humanistic reaction to a music grown doctrinaire and artificial, and the introduction of new technical theories and procedures, or the relaxation of traditional constraints. But only the transition from Renaissance to Baroque and the present transition from European to Afro-American have effected such elaborate changes of vocabulary, rhetoric and syntax that one must speak of new languages, however much each new language has retained of the old. And only these two transitions have represented so drastic a shift of esthetic base.

It is no insignificant coincidence, certainly, that the twelve-tonists, perverse, in my view, as their intentions may be, feel that their method, or doctrine, of musical composition also represents a new language. The coincidence adds importantly, if only circumstantially, to other evidence that the old language had nothing more to say, that its communicative resources could no longer yield the kind of familial evolution that had spawned the Classic and Romantic epochs.

As Ernst Křenek put it, explaining the reactionary flavor of neoclassicism as opposed to serialism, in his *Selbstdarstellung* (1948):

The new simplicity [neoclassicism], as revealed by both older and younger composers, is distinct from similar movements in the past in that it is not restricted to the simplification of structure but reaches back to a previous musical language, namely, tonality. The post-Bach primitives cannot be cited as parallels, since the musical language was not changed. It was tonal both before and after. A hypothetical parallel would have the composers of the seventeenth century, confused by Monteverdi's innovations, going back to the modal style of Palestrina.

The twelve-tonists, among whom Křenek has consistently been the most articulate of a verbose assembly, are correct, I believe, in their appreciation of the state of music at about the turn of the century as representing a rhetorical dead end; and they are also correct in relating it to a comparable situation at the close of the sixteenth century. In their own view, they did what had to be done—and, indeed, the only thing that could still be done—to safeguard the continuity of the European tradition. One could, as a dodecaphonist, or serialist, go on writing sonatas, suites, symphonies, concertos, operas and chamber music. The same musicians who played Beethoven and Wagner and Strauss could, with a bit of tortuous reorientation and a lot of hard work, play Schoenberg, Berg and Webern. The language was strange, its syntax contrived and awkward, but it could be taught to those who had grown up in the old tongue; and the hallowed institutions, at least, might still be preserved.

Their mistake has been the assumption that the composer, confronted with an evolutionary impasse, could, with the grudging acquiescence of a captive and hopeful audience and a despairing press, call the turn. While they busied themselves with rhetorical theory, the living new language was taking form all about them—but in an alien milieu. What they could not have been expected to anticipate was the decisive participation, for the first time in the history of Western music, of, respectively, a new continent and a new civilization—Africa and America. All previous transitions had taken place within the family, so to speak, and the frictions were comparable to those of contending generations. As Friedrich Blume, in his *Renaissance and Baroque Music* (1967) puts it:

The unity of every period in the history of style is relative. Each takes over an extensive heritage in stylistic forms, means of expression, species of composition, objectives and techniques that it finds ready to hand. One part of this heritage it faithfully preserves and cultivates as an antiquity worthy of respect. Another it little by little lets fall into disuse. Still others it remodels to serve its own intent. In corresponding fashion a dying epoch hands onto the next what it has created, leaving the altered spirit of the new time to make of it what it will.

Nothing of this pattern of continuity was felt in the new indigenous music of America as it began to work its way to the surface of popular consciousness in the late 1920s and early 1930s. It was there, all right, for those who chose to look for it—the scales, the harmony, the song form and the instruments—but what was new was also too garish, too shocking, too bumptious and, for the ear attuned to traditional European music, too exotic, even in the diluted form in which it was first heard by most white listeners. Hence the reluctance and the inability of those identified with the European tradition to discern or acknowledge any kinship. Appearing as it did without credentials, either of precedent or of pedigree, its validity and possible ascendancy were—and, for most people, still are—unthinkable.

This resistance has produced, significantly, a striking parallel with one of the distinctive phenomena of the transition from Renaissance to Baroque—the coexistence, for a considerable period of time, of two incompatible musical idioms. "The old style," says Bukofzer in his *Music in the Baroque Era,* "was not cast aside, but deliberately preserved as a second language, known as the *stile antico* of church music. The hitherto unchallenged unity of style disintegrated, and composers were obliged to become bilingual." If, today, we were to substitute *stile antico* and *stile moderno,* for Serious and Popular, or for Classical and Jazz, the pertinence to our own time of Bukofzer's description of coexistence in the seventeenth century would be obvious.

For most of those concerned with music, however, whether professional or amateur, the legitimacy of the comparison is compromised by the conventional view of the Serious composer as a writer of modern music. Those who wrote in the *stile antico* in the seventeenth century were militant conservatives. But so also, in my view, are today's Serious composers. Their conservatism may be masked by a fulsome profession of modernism, but what they write is addressed, however despotically, to an essentially conservative public hostile to, or ignorant of, any truly modern music. This public's taste is documented in the viable repertoire of the opera house and the concert hall. The composer in his profession of modernity, the public in its tolerance of new music that it rarely likes, and the critics in their championship of the composer's right to be heard—and to go on being heard, whether his music pleases or not—are allied in what Virgil Thomson has described, with engaging candor, as "a conspiracy to defend the faith."

Nor is their conservatism solely or even essentially musical. Basically it is institutional, concerned primarily with preserving the symbols of an established social order and with perpetuating an established catalogue of cultural virtues. Most people go to concerts and the opera today just as they go to church, sincere enough in their worship, whether of God or of Beethoven, but also savoring the respectability of their attendance and the assumption of connoisseurship.

They are hardly different, really, from those who supported Italian *opera seria* into the nineteenth century, as if there had never been a revolution in France—or a Beethoven; or from the boxholders of later generations who went on listening to vintage Italian opera, or French opera sung in Italian, in London, Paris, St. Petersburg and New York just as if there had never been a Wagner—or an industrial revolution. There were Crescentini and Catalani and Mrs. Billington to sing for them—or Grisi and Mario and Lablache, or Patti and Melba and dear Jean de Reszke—and all was right with the world.

The legitimacy of the comparison—returning to Bukofzer—is supported now, after fifty years of coexistence, by the number of composers and musicians who are becoming bilingual. Every Third Stream composition is, of course, an exercise in bilinguality, but such exercises require, as a rule, some sort of accommodation insupportable by either language if they are to achieve the fusion essential to anything that can be thought of seriously as a stream. The true bilingualists, most of them still young and working safe from critical captiousness in the commercial fields, keep the languages apart or join them in such a way that one language is predominant, drawing upon the other only for what is appropriate to the task, and assigning from the task only what is appropriate to the language.

There are many other parallels between the seventeenth century and the twentieth, and each of them is worth examination. Most obvious, perhaps, is a nearly identical reaction, in favor of intimacy and immediacy, to a music that had become too complex, too scientific, too overloaded and too remote from the natural lyrical expression of human sentiment and the natural rhythms of bodily movement. The reaction in the seventeenth century had, to be sure, been led by intellectuals, and its first composers, as Bukofzer says, tended to be bilingual. The twentieth-century reaction, as reflected in jazz, was led by nobody. But the results have been the same.

They have included, again as in the seventeenth century, and for the first time since then, a new musical terminology, suggesting a music so different from all earlier music, and different in such fundamental particulars, that a new descriptive vocabulary has had to be evolved. Throughout the Renaissance epoch, roughly from 1430 to 1570, the international language of musical terminology had been Latin. With Baroque came not only the ascendancy of the Italian musician but also the general acceptance of the Italian musician's own vocabulary for the designation of musical instruments, musical objectives, performance procedures and techniques, and so on. This Italian terminology has provided the basic international code employed by musicians everywhere, whether they speak Italian or not. For all the many modifications demonstrable in Western music during the Classic and Romantic periods, there was no change in concept, method or technique so radical as to render the traditional Italian terminology inapplicable and obsolete.

With the new American indigenous music it is quite another matter. It has not been merely that the early jazz musicians—most of them musically illiterate—were unfamiliar with traditional terminology. The Italian words, even for those musicians who knew them, were inadequate and inappropriate. And so the jazz musician, like the Italian musicians of the seventeenth century, devised his own terminology, basically English but employing new words of his own invention that are only now beginning to find their way into standard dictionaries.

American English is the common language of jazz musicians everywhere, and the singular terminology of jazz is internationally understood even by those whose command of a more commonplace English vocabulary is limited. When American jazz musicians use such terms as bop, swing, groove, cool, lead, funk, soul, riff, break, intro, segue, chorus, release, change, comp and so on, other jazz musicians know immediately what they are talking about. A German, French, Italian, Swedish, Swiss, Yugoslav, Hungarian, Polish or Japanese jazzman, reading a jazz arrangement, or original, will not be put off when he finds himself directed to play in "a medium 'Basie' groove," or to "play time freely," or to "comp changes."

So intimate is this association of terminology and art that critics writing in other languages than English, and attempting to describe what the music and the musicians have to say, can find no substitute for the jazz musician's terms, and simply throw them in, assuming that the reader himself would also use them. The result is often a hilarious hybrid where the native rather than the foreign word will appear anachronistic. Examples are easy to come by, but I was especially taken by this headline over the column of folk-record reviews in a German newspaper: "Folklore, Protest *und etwas* Beat." The review contained the following extraordinary sentence: *"Der* Beat *sänftigt sich* [moderates itself] *zum* Chanson, *waehrend* [while] *die* Folklore *mit* Beat *und* Pop *gepfeffert* [spiced] *wird."* And it added a new adjective to the German language: *bluesig!*

It remains to note one last, striking parallel between the transitions from Renaissance to Baroque and from European to Afro-American: the emergence, in each instance, of a

107

system of figured bass. The jazz musician improvises from designated chords just as Bach and Handel did, the only difference being in the conventions of chord designation. If a jazz combo were deprived of the rhythm section, and if the musician phrased the same notes in the European rather than the American manner, what you would hear would be a Baroque trio or quartet. The piano is the harpsichord, the guitar is the lute, the double bass the viola da gamba, and a saxophone or trumpet is the violin. Only the drummer is new, and even in Baroque the viola da gamba, in addition to pronouncing the bass line, also provided a pulse, or, to use the jazz musician's terminology, "played time."

The jazz musician has his own ideas of melodic variation and embellishment, but the purpose and the procedure are identical with those of the Baroque musician. The structural form favored by the jazz combo, or chamber group, today—as opposed to the theme-and-variations form favored by earlier generations of jazz musicians—is the chaconne, a series of developing improvisations over a predetermined sequence of chords, usually those of a popular tune. And most jazz band arrangements are nothing more or less than a *concerto grosso* for a variety of solo instruments. Take away the pulse and the swinging accentuation, and you have Corelli, Vivaldi and even Bach.

What is significant about all this, however, is not so much the similarity of the musical procedure as the similarity of the circumstance that produced it: a reaction against oversophistication and artificiality requiring a return to music's roots in song and dance while retaining the Western—as opposed to Oriental or African—predilection for multiple voices. It is not, therefore, that the new music has been so new in any absolute sense, either in the seventeenth century or in the twentieth; rather that it has been so vital in contrast to an older idiom that had grown obese and sclerotic.

What distinguishes the new Afro-American idiom from any previous Western music is nothing but a new concept of rhythm and phrase. But then all that the early Baroque composers did, in breaking with the Renaissance, was put a new stress to the top and bottom lines of multiple-voiced song. It seems very little in either case. But it has been felt as sufficiently radical and sufficiently offensive, at the time, to blind the traditionalist to how much of the old was still present in the new, and to excite his resistance. It has been enough, as Bukofzer says of the Baroque, "to disintegrate the unity of style."

I would prefer "idiomatic integrity" to "the unity of style," particularly as applied to the twentieth century; for Serious music already supported a variety of styles without inspiring among its adherents any sense of impending idiomatic disaster. Everyone was aware, more or less, of an alien idiom in jazz; but the categorical distinction between Serious and Popular encouraged a feeling of non-involvement and security.

The Serious composers, the Serious critics and the Serious-music community as a whole were mindful of the mistakes attributed to earlier generations in the assessment of new music. Determined not to be caught napping again, they welcomed their own new Serious music against their better judgment. Like statesmen and military men, they tended to appraise the present in terms of the past, and to make the decisions that should have been made before. And so they concentrated on the wrong novelties and drew the wrong conclusions.

One thing, indeed, musical developments since World War II have made absolutely and ironically clear [wrote an anonymous reviewer in the (London) *Times Literary Supplement* (January 4, 1968), discussing a batch of new books about modern music]:

all the battles fought on behalf of the modern movement in music—the struggle to gain Schoenberg a hearing, the strife to secure Stravinsky a place as someone other than the composer of *Firebird* and *Petrouchka*—were fought under the wrong banner. We all thought at the time that our efforts to promote the modern masters of the day were not only designed to achieve recognition for music of genius, but also to guarantee a future—a new future—for the art itself. The modern movement, if only it could be established, was the promise of a new dawn.

From our present vantage point everything looks very different and perhaps slightly disillusioning. The new dawn has turned out to be a sunset, or, if not that, then certainly a summit tinged by the rays of a traditional sun. For instead of the modern movement carrying us forward into a new period, the leaders of it now emerge as grand old men magnificently chipping away at the old, familiar veins from which their predecessors had mined their materials. As the years roll by, in fact, what seemed to divide the most significant and influential composers—Schoenberg's serial method, Stravinsky's brand of neo-classicism or Hindemith's—seem of little importance if compared with the central ambition which united them; the determination to extend and, above all, to maintain, the great tradition into which they were born.

It is probably no insignificant coincidence that about the time this article appeared, another British writer, Peter Heyworth, music critic of the London *Observer,* was documenting similar conclusions in an article, "The Fatal Sixties," for *High Fidelity* (June, 1968). Speaking of Schoenberg and Stravinsky, he said:

Each in his own way had been forced by pressure of the predicaments they had confronted to pursue parallel courses. . . . In a period of incipient disintegration, both felt the need of classical procedures to hold together scores of length and substance. In a word, whatever details may be new in this or that work, the basic cast of their music after 1918 was conservative. . . . But by their heroic efforts to keep the skies suspended, they had evaded the crisis rather than met it.

Music critics and music historians, both writers had noted earlier in their discussions, assumed that popular rejection of contemporary Serious music was simply a matter of history repeating itself, that the new composers, in due course, would be vindicated as Beethoven and Wagner, Brahms and Strauss, had all been vindicated. And both writers rather more than hinted that the time had come to acknowledge a fundamental miscalculation. But neither of them was ready to suggest that in their ignorance and rejection of contemporary Popular music, the critics and historians had, in fact, committed precisely the error that their sponsorship of the new music was designed to avoid.

History, as usual, fooled the experts. And it fooled them in the usual way. It didn't repeat. Only the experts repeated.

American Music and
the Musical
Establishment

THE CRITICS, the historians and the educators of the eighteenth and nineteenth centuries—Mattheson, Burney, Hawkins, Rochlitz, Reichardt, the Rellstabs, Schumann, Fétis,
Berlioz, Chorley, Davison, Hanslick and Newman—all had
their foibles, their shortcomings and their blind spots. They
may have been hostile or inhospitable to new music of
their own time, music that has since been hailed, possibly
incorrectly, as progressive. But they knew what the new
music was.

Our own critics, historians, musicologists and educators,
many of whom are also advisers to philanthropic foundations
and consultants to art councils, do not. For the most part,
they haven't heard it; and what they have heard they have
ignored or dismissed. They have slept soundly through—or
have gone on listening to Beethoven through—the most
turbulent century in Western music since the seventeenth.
And it is they who compose the musical Establishment. Their
performance in the assessment of the century's music, both in
their estimate of new Serious music and in their studied

112

exclusion and ignorance of what they think of as Popular music, constitutes a professional disaster.

The musical Establishment has, with significant unanimity, acted on the assumption that music, if it is to be thought respectable, must demonstrate its suitability for the concert hall and the opera house according to the conventions of a European frame of esthetic reference, including the forms, the instruments and the interpretive dogma associated with Serious, or European, music. And they have seemed to assume that any music so qualified is, therefore, respectable.

This Establishment has gaily appropriated for itself the very word *music*. Millions and millions of words have been written about "contemporary music" in the critics' Sunday columns, in musical periodicals and in books on contemporary music without a reference to jazz or to any kind of jazz-influenced Popular music. American and British magazines with such titles as *Musical Quarterly, Music & Letters, Music and Musicians, Musical Times, Musical America* (!) etc., rarely, some of them never, give any coverage to jazz. The same is true of comparable publications on the continent. Those who write about jazz in the newspapers are not "music critics." They are "jazz critics." Jazz is excluded—with some exceptions to be noted later—from the curricula of formal musical education. And in the view of the philanthropists and arts councils, jazz, disparaged by the Establishment as "a performer's art," is not included among what the same Establishment solicitously terms the "performing arts."

Even occasional benevolence tends to be hideously patronizing. *The World of Music,* for example, the quarterly journal of the International Music Council (UNESCO), devoted its Vol. 10, No. 3 (1968) issue to jazz. In an article titled, characteristically, "New Music and Jazz," the Soviet composer Edison Denissow speaks of "the direct application of jazz elements in the music of the 20th century," as if jazz were somehow not twentieth-century music. And an introduction to the contributors includes a description of Henry Pleasants as the author of books "on music and jazz."

Throughout the century, the Establishment has either ignored jazz or disdained it as an urban folk music. There was a disposition, earlier in the century, to assume that its vitality might provide raw materials, so to speak, for processing by Serious composers into Serious music. But the two idioms proved, as we have seen, to be incompatible. Nothing came of it, and the failure served only to inhibit any view of jazz as having something to do with the art of music. When various experiments with symphonic jazz and with jazz opera in the 1930s and 1940s indicated a misalliance, the Establishment washed its hands of the whole business.

Inspection and dismissal, in some quarters, were recklessly hasty, as in Aaron Copland's *Our New Music* (1941) :

The preoccupation with the popular idiom in the principal centers of jazz influence—France, Germany and England—had expended itself by the end of the twenties. The revival of interest in jazz of the so-called "hot" variety, which came into vogue around 1935 under the name of swing, has, thus far, at any rate, had little effect on serious music. . . . Our *jazz interlude* [italics added] had no permanent effect on contemporary music's trend away from romanticism. It was a temporary interest, similar to the interest in the primitive arts and crafts of aboriginal people in the fields of sculpture and painting.

For Copland, then, jazz bemused the Serious composer as an exotic curiosity during an interlude between romanticism and neoclassicism. Similarly, Friedrich Herzfeld, in his *Musica Nova* (1954), is interested in jazz only insofar as its influence has been perceptible in Serious music. He identifies

114

the high point of this influence in Křenek's *Jonny spielt auf* (1927). The charms, he concludes, "faded rapidly. Today the sounds of jazz seem yellowed and dated, and they are seldom heard in art music. The influence of jazz, especially of rhythm, was indisputably great, but it was, on the whole, a passing fashion."

Norman Demuth, late Professor of Composition at the Royal Academy of Music in London, in *Musical Trends in the 20th Century* (1952), devoted only a single page of 344 pages to jazz, just enough to echo Copland and Herzfeld: "The influence of so-called jazz has penetrated the concert hall, and its scintillating rhythms have found a place in the music of one or two composers who have had their minds on higher things."

Others have written as if jazz did not exist, among them Paul Henry Lang, in the 1,030 pages of whose *Music in Western Civilization* the word does not appear. There is no reference to the American songwriter, either, although a brief dissertation on dance music and operetta does include this not especially enigmatic statement: "as long as there are no composers to follow in their footsteps [of Pepusch, Hiller and Lortzing] and in those of Monsigny, Sullivan and the French composers we shall mention presently, the popular lyric stage will be dominated by products coming from the artistic gutter of the metropolises."

Arthur Honegger, neither in his *Je suis compositeur* (1951), nor in his *Incantations aux fossiles* (1948), makes any reference to jazz. Nor does Roger Sessions in *The Musical Experience* (1950), although his book includes a twenty-page chapter on "Music in the World Today." H. H. Stueckenschmidt, in *Neue Musik* (1951), in seven pages devoted to *"Neue Musik in Amerika,"* makes only a passing reference to Woody Herman, Stan Kenton and George

Gershwin. Jacques Chailley, in *40,000 Years of Music* (1961), a book subtitled "Man in Search of Music," did not find jazz.

It matters little whether the writer is European or American. John Tasker Howard, as late as 1946, in the third edition of *Our American Music,* devoted just three and a half of 692 pages to jazz, and the only Negro musicians he mentioned were Louis Armstrong, Count Basie and Fats Waller. Jacques Barzun, in *Music in American Life* (1956), acknowledging the worldwide dissemination of jazz, writes: "No wonder that some observers have been misled into thinking that jazz was, indeed, the one musical idiom expressive of our age and used it as a battering ram to destroy the pretensions of other kinds of composers."

Ernst Bacon, of Syracuse University, was so taken with the acuity of Barzun's insight that he used it as a motto for the chapter on jazz in his own *Words on Music* (1960). Jazz would, he thought, "like any kind of popular or less sophisticated music (as distinguished from what we so condescendingly call 'art music') find its way into the larger music as did the waltz, the polonaise, the minuet, the gigue, the sarabande or the folk song in the past." Mr. Bacon has a curious view of the character of jazz. It has, he says, "its own special sphere, a unique kind of intoxication and parody." He is obviously delighted with this formulation, for after acknowledging that "jazz has become far and away the most authentic musical speech of America," he reiterates it, offering jazz "the crown of parody and intoxicant irresponsibility." Actually, he is echoing Barzun, who had said: "Everything it is associated with suggests repetition and the excitement that precedes narcosis."

Gilbert Chase, in the revised second edition of *America's Music* (1966), does better. Although he devotes only 25 of 692 pages to jazz, his discussion is knowledgeable and sympathetic. But he is not ready to sponsor its admission to the club. "If jazz," he writes in his preface, "may be regarded as our most original and far-reaching contribution to the world's music, this should not blind us to the fact that our 'serious music,' or fine-art music, is at present capable of holding its own with most contemporary music that is being composed anywhere."

Chase's suggestion that jazz "may be regarded as our most original and far-reaching contribution to the world's music" would hardly be contested by most Establishment spokesmen. But neither would the same spokesmen concede that even this "most original and far-reaching contribution" entitled jazz to be taken Seriously. Typical, probably, is the attitude reflected in *Music in History,* third edition (1966), by Howard D. McKinney and W. R. Anderson.

"Whether we are reluctant to admit it or not," the authors tell us, "the outstanding contribution which the United States so far has made to twentieth century music has been in the popular field—specifically (1) jazz, (2) what has come to be known as 'pop' music and (3) works written for the musical theater." They also concede that "America has produced few, if any, serious composers of first-rate importance and international significance." And yet, of 55 pages devoted to American music, 35 are devoted to contemporary American Serious music and only three to jazz.

Arnold Shaw, in his chapter on "Popular Music from Minstrel Songs to Rock 'n' Roll," included in *One Hundred Years of Music in America* (1961), edited by Paul Henry Lang, senses something sinister in the exclusion of jazz from acceptance as art. "It is hard to discover," he writes, "the purpose of the separation, although in the minds of those who seek to perpetuate it there is probably the same fear of the hybrid as among those favoring segregation."

I doubt it. There is fear of the hybrid, to be sure, but no

conscious awareness of a racial threat, and no *witting* racial exclusion. The Establishment is concerned with the preservation of what it regards, sincerely, I think, as immutable cultural criteria. The black musician is welcomed, and sometimes enjoys even preferential treatment, if only he will devote himself to European music, or to music conceived as a perpetuation of a European cultural heritage. The Establishment and its institutions are designed and determined to restrain musical evolution within a prescribed channel. What takes place outside the channel, or seeks to alter its course, is simply ignored or outlawed.

The black jazz musician interprets this as racial discrimination, or, more accurately, as cultural discrimination. But it is, in fact, racial only in the sense that the new musical idiom is Afro-American rather than Euro-American. And the Establishment does not think in those terms. In its own view, the Establishment is protecting culture from Popular pollution and discriminating only between Art and Entertainment. And it can point to the fact that the white jazz musician is discriminated against just as rigidly as the black.

Most members of the Establishment, probably, sense an alien presence, and they react, as I have suggested earlier, according to Robert Ardrey's "territorial imperative." But the reaction is instinctive rather than tactical. Even those who have qualms about contemporary Serious music, and who have noted the reactionary flavor, remain oblivious to the implications—even when the true state of affairs is hinted at by club members in good standing.

"This radical revision of our approach to the history of twentieth century music," observed the anonymous commentator of the (London) *Times Literary Supplement* in the article cited at the close of the preceding chapter, referring to the dawn that had turned out to be a sunset, "has not

118

yet found its way into the text-books, and without it what we read is necessarily misleading and muddled. All too often, in the absence of a real perspective, we have as substitute a mass of detail—flitting from composer to composer, from style to style, from school to school—which strikes one as hugely irrelevant and totally unilluminating."

Actually, the revision is closer to finding its way into the textbooks than our reviewer thinks; and important evidence is right there in one of the books that were under review. The *Times Literary Supplement* man offers *Music in the 20th Century* (1966), by William Austin, Professor of Music at Cornell University, as "a painful case of not seeing the wood for the trees," and then himself misses the wood by discursive nit-picking about Austin's treatment of some minor Serious composers, while failing to note what is truly remarkable about this book: Austin, instead of conventionally identifying two main idiomatic influences—dodecaphonic and neoclassical—identifies four: Schoenberg, Stravinsky, Bartók—and jazz!

Austin, if not his critic, knew perfectly well what was remarkable in his own performance:

To place at the center, with Schoenberg, Bartók and Stravinsky, not another individual, but another style—jazz [he writes in his preface], risks repelling some. But there is room to hope that this recognition of jazz may make evident an extended and strengthened consensus. If most readers interested in Schoenberg, Bartók and Stravinsky are only slightly interested in jazz, they may still be supposed willing to entertain the possibility that some jazz deserves their continuing study, too, or at least to indulge the author's hope even if his evidence leaves them unconverted. And if his hope is realized, they will sooner or later agree that jazz belongs at the center, that Armstrong, Ellington,

119

Parker and the rest together deserve the kind of attention given to each of the greatest three composers individually.

Austin is treading gingerly here, as well he might; but he is less apprehensively apologetic than Leonard Bernstein in the latter's homage to pop in the preface to *The Infinite Variety of Music* (1966) :

I confess, freely though unhappily, that at this moment, as of this writing, God forgive me, I have far more pleasure in following the musical adventure of Simon & Garfunkel, or of The Association singing "Along Comes Mary" than I have in most of what is being written now by the whole community of "avant-garde" composers. . . . Pop music seems to be the only area where there is to be found unabashed vitality, the fun of invention, the feeling of fresh air. Everything else suddenly seems old-fashioned; electronic music, serialism, chance music—they have already acquired the musty odor of academicism. . . .

And Austin is probably unduly optimistic in what appears to be an assumption that "most readers interested in Schoenberg" are even "only slightly interested in jazz," as also in his hope that they will "sooner or later agree that jazz belongs at the center." Such general recognition is, in my opinion, at least a generation off, and by that time most of what has been vital in jazz throughout the past twenty years will have qualified for academic attention as history.

He devotes only 36 of 537 pages to jazz, which is miserly for a phenomenon to which he attaches such importance. But what he says in those few pages is perceptive, well-informed and to the point. While never quite equating it with Serious music, he accepts, nevertheless, the jazz musician's insistence on a distinction between jazz and Popular, and he even notes the quality of some music unabashedly Popular, although in singling out Ray Charles as an example of how good rock 'n' roll can be, he fails to make the essential distinction between rock 'n' roll and rhythm-and-blues. In fact, the term rhythm-and-blues does not occur in his otherwise sophisticated text.

His documentation of the invention and the intuitive structural genius of both Louis Armstrong and Charlie Parker is admirable, and it should help to refute the Serious-music community's complacent dismissal of jazz as trivial music. But it fails to identify and emphasize those characteristics that distinguish jazz from the music of his three principals—Schoenberg, Stravinsky and Bartók—and from the totality of European, or Serious, music, including American Serious music. All he offers is evidence that the best of jazz is comparable in its structural procedures to Schoenberg, Stravinsky and Bartók—or at least worthy of being mentioned in the same breath. And that, God knows, is something, coming from a professor.

(Austin's book is dedicated, incidentally, to Donald Jay Grout, Professor of Musicology at Cornell, whose own *A History of Western Music* (1960) devotes five and a half lines to jazz, just 62 out of 22,500 words expended on music of the twentieth century. "Another feature of the twentieth century," says Grout, "was the rise of jazz in the United States of America, a development largely independent of the more pretentious forms. Jazz has attained a *mystique* of its own and attracted a large number of devoted followers in all countries. Its influence on other types of music has been evident from time to time since about 1918.")

Another academician who has appreciated the genius of the jazz musician, and who has not been afraid to commit his appreciation to writing, is Wilfrid Mellers, Professor of Music at the University of York. In a book titled *Music in a*

New Found Land (1964), he tells us in his preface that jazz "has produced composers such as Ellington and composing-improvisers such as Louis Armstrong, Charlie Parker and Miles Davis, whose work is certainly of greater creative significance than that of (literally) hundreds of art composers whose music is performed intermittently, if infrequently, in the concert hall." But Mellers, too, subsequently, covers his flanks, speaking of "a solo flute hovering between the world of art and that of jazz." Part II of his book, from which this line is drawn, is headed, moreover: "The World of Art and the World of Commerce: The Folk Song of the Asphalt Jungle."

Both Austin and Mellers reflect an incipient shift in the academic position on jazz. It is not precipitate, but it is perceptible; and acceleration in the next decade would seem to be inevitable, spurred from outside the senior Establishment by student and junior faculty initiative, and from inside by an increasing awareness of the sterility and academicism of contemporary Serious composition.

This sterility, especially, has become a serious matter for higher music education, since the graduate composer, failing to find a welcome in the outside world, tends to fall back on the campus, where, with all the blessings of title and tenure, he can continue until retirement to pass on to others the not very exacting discipline of composing what few want to hear. Small wonder that Peter Davis, New York music critic of the London *Times,* discussing New York's musical avant-garde and the general public's indifference to it in the issue of December 29, 1967, could say:

Few composers are evidently distressed by the situation as they retreat farther and farther into the sanctuary of the university, surfacing occasionally for a concert, either here or in one of the country's larger urban areas. American colleges and conservatories, in fact, no longer "turn out" composers—"turn in" would be a more accurate description. Since there is no professional demand for his wares, the young avant-gardist simply stays at his university or moves to another. What will happen when swelling music departments reach the saturation point should be a sobering prospect.

Igor Stravinsky, in an interview with the *New York Review of Books* (March 14, 1968), made similar observations and reached similar conclusions: "The Ph.D. composers must compose for themselves last, as well as first, since *they* are their only audience. *What* they compose, in further subtraction to being unuseful, unsought—except by their own logging enterprises—and uninteresting, is also largely unprintable, partly because of the minuteness of sales, partly because it is part of the game that each new opus has to have a new notation." In return for the university's feeding, clothing and maintaining him, Stravinsky continued, that kind of composer breeds "by conversion and through technical analyses . . . a great many more of his kind."

Even more serious, in the United States, are the demands of students for education in a professionally viable contemporary music and the demands of the junior and senior high schools for teachers equipped to satisfy the students' enthusiasm for something more than formal musical education. That these demands have not previously been either sufficiently loud or sufficiently insistent to provoke action is easily explained. The education has actually been provided *outside the approved educational curriculum!* The results of this extracurricular education, however, have been so spectacular, and the student response has been so enthusiastic, that the educational system can no longer wholly ignore it.

At the center of this activity is an institution known euphemistically as the "stage band." Other terms for the same thing are "workshop band" and "lab band." Whatever the term, it is actually a fifteen- to twenty-piece jazz band, the euphemism being imposed by a middle-class, middle-aged abhorrence of the word "jazz," especially in the Midwest and Southwest, where the movement, both in the high schools and in the colleges and universities, has flourished.

There are no precise data on the number of these bands, but reasonable estimates of the junior and senior high school bands run between 10,000 and 12,000, while college and university bands are thought to number upwards of 400. In addition to their local appearances, about a thousand of the junior and senior high school bands take part annually in some sixty regional competitive stage-band festivals. For the college and university bands there is a series of regional festivals culminating in the Intercollegiate Jazz Festival in May or June.

As is true, also, of the American college and university symphony orchestras and choruses, the quality of the best of the bands approaches that of the finest professional organizations and is superior to any but the finest. Outstanding in recent years have been the bands of North Texas State University, the University of Illinois, and Indiana University, all of which have been sent abroad by the State Department, and Ohio University and San Fernando Valley State College bands, winner and runner-up, respectively, of the Intercollegiate Jazz Festival of 1967. Again, as in the case of the student symphony orchestras, players in these bands often go directly from the campus into top professional organizations.

The telltale difference between the orchestras, choruses and opera workshops on the one hand, and the bands or combos on the other, is that participation for the one is part of the curriculum and earns degree credits, while for the other—with some exceptions, notably Indiana University, the University of Miami and North Texas State—it is extracurricular and earns no credits. In one large Southwestern university, for example, credits are given for participation in the school's famous marching band, but none for participation in its almost equally famous jazz band.

The extent of support given these bands varies from school to school, depending upon such unstable factors as the musical predilections of deans and administrators and the initiative and ability of individual faculty members and students. Only in rare instances, such as Indiana and North Texas State, is the band a part of, or under the supervision of, the university school of music, with credit given for jazz study. And only at North Texas and the University of Miami is jazz a music major leading to the degree of Bachelor of Music.

The most significant aspect of stage-band activity in the past decade has been the development of student composer-arrangers. School jazz bands, before World War II, were largely extracurricular offshoots of school concert or marching bands, playing for dances and using stock arrangements. After the war, many alumni of the big bands of the swing era went into the schools as music directors, coaching jazz bands extracurricularly and, usually, voluntarily, and introducing them to the more sophisticated arrangements of the famous bands of the time. A high percentage of the compositions and arrangements played by college and university bands today, if not by the high school bands, is the work of students themselves, sometimes representing extracurricular initiative by composition majors in the schools of music.

An important element in this phenomenon has been the

contribution of professional jazz musicians to the festivals, where they act as judges and clinicians, and to the National Stage Band Camps, where they act as instructors and advisers in composing, playing, organizing, and so on. These summer camps offer a week of intensive study at university campuses in various parts of the country, award one hour's credit to all students and enjoy university support to the extent that the required facilities are made available on a rental basis.

There is something amiss, obviously, in an educational system that provides instruction in a kind of composition for which there is little professional demand and in a kind of playing or singing where the professional opportunities are limited, but which will not provide it for a kind of composition and a kind of performance in which the professional demand is intense. In the still-fashionable view of the educational Establishment, however, such composition and such performance are "commercial" and, therefore, unworthy.

A change in this view is inevitable; and it is, in fact, already evident. Not only Indiana University, North Texas State and the University of Miami, but also Tulane University, the University of Texas and now, most importantly, the Eastman School of Music in Rochester and the Philadelphia Musical Academy give this instruction in degree-credit courses. There are certainly others, and there will be more, particularly with the impetus to be expected from the acceptance of the National Association of Jazz Educators into the Music Educators National Conference at the latter's biennial convention in Seattle in March, 1968.

This is encouraging, but the overall situation remains disgraceful. I have been assured (1967) by the National Association of Schools of Music that *few* university and college schools of music and accredited conservatories give instruction in jazz, and that the student jazz groups, *i.e.,* big bands, combos, etc., exist *as a rule* outside the framework of the schools of music. Those concerned with public school music advise me that the comparable situation in secondary education is even worse.

The young American musician, in other words, desiring to be educated in his own music, must, *as a rule,* look for it outside the educational system. If he will only devote himself to the older disciplines of European, or Serious, music, education is his for the asking. There is no harm in such education, and doubtless much good; but the young musician attracted to a more contemporary music gets more Serious instruction than he needs, and some of it, inevitably, inhibits his growth and progress in his own music. It also means, if he pursues his jazz studies on the outside, an ill-adjusted distribution of time.

Much the same may be said of music education in other countries. In England the establishment of a three-year course in "Jazz and Light Music" at the Music Centre in Leeds, the first full-time course of its kind in the country, may indicate the beginning of a breakthrough, and the London Youth Jazz Orchestra has been given logistical support by the Westminster Youth Office. Much emphasis is now given to jazz in the musicology curriculum of the University of London, and courses in jazz and pop have recently been added to the curriculum at the University of York. But, as the London *Times* jazz critic, Miles Kington, put it in an article on May 1, 1967: "It is a reflection of the vast inertia that exists on the educational side that most of the initiative must still come from the world of jazz." The Gulbenkian Foundation's report on music education in England, published in 1965 as *Making Musicians,* characteristically does not mention jazz.

The arguments brought forward most frequently by Establishment spokesmen—those spokesmen, that is, who have progressed beyond the "unthinkable!" stage—to rationalize the exclusion of jazz are that (1) there is no demand for it and (2) jazz cannot be taught. The number of those participating in high school and university jazz bands and combos, and the high standard of their performance, would seem to be an adequate refutation of both arguments. It is more likely that students interested in jazz education are simply not accustomed to look for it in the accredited schools of music; and they are probably well aware that the schools are ill equipped to teach it.

There is, moreover, the more concrete evidence, both of demand and of the fact that jazz can be taught, provided by the Berklee School of Music in Boston, the only music school in the world dedicated to the education of the jazz musician and composer-arranger. As of this writing, Berklee is in its twenty-fifth year, with an enrollment of 650 students from nineteen countries and a faculty of 75. It has recently received the approval of the State of Massachusetts to award degrees in music.

The policies of the foundations and art councils toward jazz follow the Establishment pattern of exclusion. In neither the Rockefeller *Panel Report on The Performing Arts: Problems and Prospects* (1965) nor in the William Jack Baumol and W. G. Bowen study, *Performing Arts—The Economic Dilemma* (1966) is there even a passing reference to jazz, and Alvin Toffler overlooks it in his *The Culture Consumers* (1964).

The National Endowment of the Arts, according to a spokesman for the National Foundation of the Arts and Humanities, "has no programs involving jazz at the present time [1967]." A jazz committee was added to the Music Panel in 1968. The Lincoln Center for the Performing Arts has no one from jazz among its officers and directors, or on the Lincoln Center Council, and neither its Festival '67 nor the Performing Arts Convocation had any jazz participation. The Contemporary Music Project of Creativity in Music Education, a fund-granting committee of the Music Educators National Conference, was giving no funds to jazz composer-arrangers as of 1966. The New York State Council on the Arts awarded $11,250 to Jazz Interactions for a program of jazz concert-lectures in the public schools in 1967–68. The Martha Baird Rockefeller Fund, which has given valuable help to hundreds of young Serious musicians quietly and wisely, "makes no grants to jazz musicians [1967]."

The Ford Foundation and the Rockefeller Foundation have given more than a hundred million dollars to symphony orchestras and opera enterprises and to projects designed to promote the welfare and prosperity of the Serious composer, but nothing, except three Ford Foundation grants totaling $156,000 to the Jazz Archive of Tulane University, to jazz. The Guggenheim Foundation, which has given hundreds of research grants to Serious musicians, has given grants to Marshall Stearns for *The Story of Jazz* (1956), to Teo Macero and William O. Smith, who work in both the Serious and the jazz idioms, and now, finally (1967), to Ornette Coleman. The choice of Coleman was thought to be of dubious propriety by many in the jazz community; and his project, a composition for the Philadelphia Chamber Orchestra, reflects the Establishment view that in order to be considered worthy of institutional philanthropy a jazz musician must associate himself with Serious music.

In Great Britain, also in 1967, jazz could celebrate a modest breakthrough when the Arts Council granted an award of 800 pounds to Graham Collier, jazz bassist and composer-arranger and, incidentally, an alumnus of the

Berklee School of Music. The composition "Workpoints" resulting from this grant was well received, and in 1968 similar awards went to Mike Westbrook and Mike Taylor.

There is, it should be noted, a tendency in the Establishment to think of all jazz musicians as commercial and rich. Some jazz musicians have prospered, just as Artur Rubinstein, Van Cliburn and Maria Callas have prospered; but few of them are more prosperous than the average Serious musician, and most of them are not prosperous at all. Nor do they have any of the security conceded to the symphony orchestra musician as a right—a full year's employment, pension plan, etc. Nor do many of them, and least of all the older Negro musicians, have any refuge in the academic world.

The consequences of the jazz musician's hazardous and precarious existence may be read in the appalling roll of premature deaths: Mildred Bailey, Shorty Baker, Bix Beiderbecke, Bunny Berigan, Clifford Brown, Charlie Christian, Nat King Cole, John Coltrane, Tadd Dameron, Eric Dolphy, the Dorsey brothers, Ziggy Elman, Herschel Evans, Irving Fazola, John Graas, Jimmy Harrison, Stan Hasselgard, Billie Holiday, Bobby Jaspar, Billy Kyle, Tommy Ladnier, Scott LaFaro, Booker Little, Jimmie Lunceford, Wes Montgomery, Fats Navarro, Charlie Parker, Oscar Pettiford, Bud Powell, Otis Redding, Django Reinhardt, Art Tatum, Frank Teschemacher, Dave Tough, Fats Waller, Little Walter, Dinah Washington, Chick Webb, Lester Young, and so on and on and on.

Musicians all—good musicians and excellent musicians, among them a genius or two. Within the musical Establishment their deaths—from tuberculosis, cancer, cirrhosis, drug addiction, heart disease and automobile accidents—were unnoted and unmourned. For even the most famous of them, as far as the Establishment was concerned, were merely Popular musicians.

130

Social rejection; exclusion from education in his own idiom, either as student or as teacher; withholding of official (other than State Department) sponsorship and the benefits of institutional philanthropy; denial of any kind of economic or professional security; and, finally, ignorance of, and indifference to, his achievements—such has been the Establishment's appreciation of the jazz musician and of our "most original and far-reaching contribution to the world's music"!

"One can reject jazz," wrote Kurt Honolka, the Stuttgart musicologist, in *Musik in unserer Zeit* (1960), "but only the blind and the deaf will ignore it."

He was right about that. But he might have chosen less exculpatory adjectives.

Bop and the New Jazz

WITH THE Serious music community now fitfully aware of an impending crisis, implicit in the failure of Serious composers to produce any considerable amount of music that any considerable number of the community's members find esthetically rewarding, jazz is experiencing a very severe crisis of its own. In discussing this crisis, I use *jazz* as the jazz musician uses it in dissociating his own from Popular music.

It is essentially a crisis of identity, inherent in the phenomenon of a forceful new idiom incapable of accommodation within an older European idiom, the latter blessed with every advantage of prestige, position and place. The jazz musician of the late 1930s was both popular and successful; but neither his popularity nor his success could be wholly satisfactory. His popularity encouraged the conventional view of jazz as merely Popular music. Some jazz musicians knew better; and it seemed to them, therefore, that their success was earned under false colors. They were being rewarded as entertainers for what they knew to be an artistic accomplishment.

Their reaction has been manifested in two basic trends in

132

modern jazz: toward the European, or Serious, idiom on the one hand, in the form of composition and sophisticated arrangement; and away from it on the other, in the form of a new and more advanced kind of improvisation. Expressed in other terms, the one trend has been to seek respectability by attempting to reconcile jazz with European concepts of composition; the other to stress, advance and refine the improvisational techniques that have, from the earliest beginnings, been an essential and distinguishing characteristic of jazz.

There was, in any case, no escaping Serious music, nor the fashionable view that Serious music, even new Serious music, was, by definition and categorization, better than jazz. And so, in the pursuit of status, those jazz musicians who were versed in Serious music, or who could become versed, brought its techniques to jazz, while others, accepting jazz on its own terms, set out to make it more serious without, at the same time, making it more European.

None of this happened precisely according to plan or design. The jazz band of the late 1930s had already attained a level of organization and virtuosity where further progress implied a complexity beyond the capacity of musicians left to their own devices. The so-called "head arrangement" no longer sufficed. A new level of sophistication was required; and it was provided by a new kind of musician known initially as "arranger" and subsequently, as his contribution increased in importance and originality, as "composer-arranger." Improvisation, at the same time, had reached a barrier beyond which lay a new level of invention.

For the new breed of composer-arranger it was not simply a matter of scoring for the big-name bands. The popularity of the idiom in the late 1930s had brought with it a requirement for a more authentic sound in every area of Popular music. Jazz had to be made accessible to jobbing musicians who were readers rather than improvisers or ear players. At the top of the arranging profession were the men who became identified with such bands as those of Duke Ellington, Jimmie Lunceford, Chick Webb, Count Basie, Benny Goodman, Tommy Dorsey, Harry James, Glenn Miller, Claude Thornhill, Woody Herman, Stan Kenton, and so on. At the bottom were those who turned out stock arrangements for dance bands.

Among the best known and most highly esteemed of the composer-arrangers have been Ralph Burns, Benny Carter, Duke Ellington, Gil Evans, Bill Finegan, Neal Hefti, Fletcher and Horace Henderson, Bill Holman, Quincy Jones, Gerry Mulligan, Jimmy Mundy, Oliver Nelson, Chico O'Farrill, Johnny Richards, Pete Rugolo, Eddie Sauter and Billy Strayhorn. Most of them began as executant musicians, or sidemen, with name bands, entering the composing field by writing for the bands in which they played, going on from there to writing for other bands, orchestrating Broadway musicals, doing backings for singers, composing underscores for motion pictures, TV serials, radio and TV commercials, etc. Their activity and production have been prodigious, the quality of their work often high, their influence on the evolution of Western music in the twentieth century incalculable and indelible.

From their work, and from the work of many more, have emerged new conventions of instrumentation, notation, compositional procedure and performance; and these may be studied not only in their compositions and arrangements, but also in such textbooks as William Russo's *Composing for Jazz Orchestra* (1961), George Russell's *The Lydian Concept of Tonal Organization* (1953) and Henry Mancini's *Sounds and Scores* (1962). Among today's composers, of any category, the composer-arrangers are the true professionals in the sense that the composer of the eighteenth century, attached to court or church, was a professional.

But for all their considerable accomplishments, and for all their not uncommon prosperity, they have suffered the frustrations of those who move back and forth between two worlds, firmly rooted in neither the one nor the other—and the hazards of the tightrope walker, too, never quite sure whether the next step may drop them into something more Serious than is tolerable to jazz, or into a kind of jazz composition where the composer-arranger abandons control to the performer.

The middle ground where they live most purposefully and most usefully is a kind of composition that provides organization and development of musical ideas while still leaving to the performers the elbow room for initiative that is essential to jazz musicianship. The severest temptation, particularly for the conservatory-trained, is to overcompose. Any work so intricate that it requires a conductor's constant attention is unlikely to achieve the exultant momentum characteristic of a jazz ensemble at its best.

But regardless of the accomplishment, it remains a middle ground. In the eyes of the Serious-music community, the composer-arrangers are not quite composers, since they do not, as a rule, write music for concert performance by symphony orchestras, or for opera companies, or choruses or string quartets. And in the eyes of the jazz purist they have a commercial taint. Their most promising field of activity today is the motion-picture underscore, and we shall have a closer look at some of these musicians in the chapter on "The Lyric Theater."

Well-known and admired as these composer-arrangers are in professional circles, they are not the musicians whom the outside world associates with jazz in the midcentury. Nor

135

have the bands for which they write dominated the jazz scene. Small groups and individual virtuosos have set the new styles. The big names have been Charlie Parker, Dizzy Gillespie, Miles Davis, Thelonious Monk, John Lewis, Charles Mingus, Kenny Clarke, Sonny Rollins and John Coltrane. And the decisive style has been bebop, or bop, hatched by the older of these musicians at Minton's Playhouse in Harlem in 1940–41. Few phenomena in the evolution of Western music have been so easy to pinpoint as to place, time and the individuals concerned. Only the Florentine Camerata, meeting at the home of Count Bardi at the end of the sixteenth century and laying the foundations of Italian opera, can be cited as a historical parallel.

Both the coterie at Minton's and the Camerata represented a radical and premeditated break with tradition, the former revolting against the artificiality of sixteenth-century polyphony, the latter against the jazz musician's dependence, for his working materials, upon the harmonic structure of the Popular song. The consequence, in the latter instance, was the divorce of jazz and Popular music. For the first time, Western music was to have not one kind of Serious music but two, a duality complicated by the defensive monotheism of the Serious-music community and by the inability of the modern jazz musician to exorcise the memory of his long and prosperous association with Popular music.

What distinguished bop from earlier forms of jazz was its defiance of conventional harmonic and melodic patterns. Where jazz had formerly concentrated on the melodic elaboration and ornamentation of a more or less familiar tune over the chords associated with that tune, bop altered the chords and distorted the melody accordingly. There were also rhythmic and accentual refinements and dislocations. When a group of bop musicians had finished with a given tune it would be unrecognizable even to its composer. The musicians sometimes acknowledged the distortion by renaming the pieces, a classic example being the emergence of "Ornithology" from "How High the Moon."

To the musicians who started it all, this was a liberating movement. They have been among the most accomplished and imaginative musicians of the century, and already in the late 1930s they, and many more, were growing tired of the traditional and predictable harmonic and melodic procedures of jazz. Devices that had been bold and decisive in the youthful exuberance of Bechet, Armstrong and Ellington had already become clichés. Every jazz musician knew them, and even inferior jazz musicians could use them. The group at Minton's wanted to break out of the groove. They also wanted to separate the men from the boys.

The movement was not, in other words, merely liberating. It was also exclusive. As Dizzy Gillespie has said of the early sessions at Minton's:

There were always some cats showing up there who couldn't blow at all but would take six or seven choruses to prove it. . . . On afternoons before a session, [Thelonious] Monk and I began to work out some complex variations on chords and the like and we used them at night to scare away the no-talent guys. After a while we got more and more interested in what we were doing as music and, as we began to explore more and more, our music evolved.

How this music sounded, and the effect it had upon other jazz musicians, has been described by John S. Wilson, jazz critic of *The New York Times*, in his book, *Jazz: The Transition Years, 1940–1960* (1966), from which the above was taken:

He [Parker] expressed himself through a kaleidoscope of surprises, mixing long and short melodic lines, simple rhythms and complex ones, legato with staccato, full-bodied tone with thin shrillness. His rhythmic accents sometimes fell on the beats as expected, at other times between beats. . . . At the same time, both he and Gillespie refused to be hemmed in by the usual construction of a melody, cutting through bar-lines and other divisions of a tune with streams of notes that might break off just as unexpectedly as they had been launched. It was an attack that often had a shattering effect on musicians encountering it for the first time. Dave Tough, one of the few swing era musicians who made the adjustment to the new music, remembered with awe his first hearing of the Dizzy Gillespie–Oscar Pettiford group on Fifty-second street in 1944. "As we walked in," Tough reported, "these cats snatched up their horns and blew. One would stop all of a sudden and another would start for no reason at all. We never could tell when a chorus was supposed to begin or end. Then they quit all at once and walked off the stand. It scared us."

Dave Tough and his friends were scared because, as young and perceptive jazz musicians, they sensed the implications of what they had just heard. The ordinary layman was simply baffled; and the old-time jazz fan and most old-time jazz musicians were outraged. This was not jazz, they said, and it never would be. Typical was Louis Armstrong: "They want to carve everyone because they're so full of malice. All they want to do is show you up and any old way will do as long as it's different from the way you played it before. So you get all them weird chords which don't mean nothing. . . ." Both Benny Goodman and Tommy Dorsey saw in the new movement a catastrophe.

In terms of jazz as a Popular music, Goodman and Dorsey

were right enough. And many today might be tempted to cite the noisome fulminations of the jazz avant-garde and the diminishing audience for jazz as proof that they were right absolutely. But this would be like citing the Schoenberg-Berg-Webern serial blight to prove that Hanslick had been absolutely right about Wagner. It would be to discount twenty-five years during which bop enjoyed an enormous national and international following and produced a score or so of extraordinary musicians, just as Wagner's innovations still yielded Strauss, Bruckner, Wolf and Mahler, and even Debussy and Ravel, before the vein of chromatic harmony and eloquent orchestration was exhausted.

It would also be to discount the many offshoots of bop, combining certain bop characteristics and procedures with a kind of jazz more readily accessible to the layman and more congenial to many jazz musicians—West Coast, cool, progressive, Afro-Cuban, etc. One does not think of Oscar Peterson, Bill Evans, Erroll Garner, Dave Brubeck, Stan Getz, Gerry Mulligan, Bob Brookmeyer, Billy Taylor and Charlie Byrd as specifically bop stylists; but it would seem to be a generalization worth risking that none of these admirable musicians would have played as he does, or did, had there never been such a thing as bop.

Stylistic fragmentation has, indeed, been one of the decisive consequences of bop, reflecting the tendency of many individual musicians to choose from the innovations and discoveries of the boppers those devices that appealed to them and seemed susceptible of processing into something congenial to a wider audience. This derivative and eclectic exploitation has excited bitter resentment among the inner circle, and it has become almost axiomatic that any jazz musician who courts and wins a large lay public will be reviled and his music dismissed as "not jazz." "If you're in jazz and more than ten people like you," flutist Herbie Mann has observed, "you're labeled commercial." Familiar examples have been Dave Brubeck and George Shearing.

At the root of this tormented history is the reluctance of society as a whole to accept the jazz musician socially, and of the musical community as a whole to accept him on equal terms with the Serious musician. Denied acceptance by the musical elite, he formed an elite of his own—a model of any exclusive grouping in any society anywhere, idealistic, self-satisfied and disdainful of the outside world, protecting itself against intrusion by constantly changing codes of expression and behavior.

Ironically, and perhaps inevitably, the attitudes of the bop musician with respect to the artist's place in society have been precisely those of the Serious-music elite that refused to let him in. All the familiar and fashionable cultural superstitions were embraced, the relevant taboos observed. The Artist stands above, and must be independent of, the public. Only Artists are qualified to pass judgment on fellow Artists. The public has a solemn obligation to listen, to render homage and to pay. It is not the Artist's business to please the public; and any Artist who tries to do so is Compromising His Integrity, Prostituting His Art, Selling Out and Going Commercial. Entertainment is beneath the true Artist's calling. And so on.

Bop musicians were encouraged in these adolescent attitudes by a new school of young jazz critics sufficiently familiar with musical history to know that Beethoven and Wagner had made arrogant noises, but ignorant, apparently, of how well both Beethoven and Wagner served their public throughout the better part of their lives—and unaware, too, of the extent to which Beethoven and Wagner represented exceptional cases and exceptional circumstances.

These young critics were, to be sure, merely aping the attitudes of their colleagues on the Serious side who had been many years ahead of them in subscribing to the Cult of the Artist and in defaulting their proper role as spokesmen for the lay public. To anyone experienced in Serious-music criticism, most jazz criticism was—and still is—a parody of remembered nonsense. All the dreary rituals of Serious-music criticism have been assiduously rehearsed, including the quest of originality, the detection of imitation, the analysis of style and attribution of influences, the romance of the Artist Who Bucks the Tide, and so on, with the critic eager to be identified with the discovery of new genius, and with the musician searching for the new departure that would attract the critic's attention.

It took European music two hundred years, beginning in the seventeenth century, to reach this stage of decadence; but then professional criticism dates only from the turn of the nineteenth century. Jazz reached it in thirty years. This has been due, in part, to the pressures imposed upon the musical artist by the phenomenon of instant and universal communication, which renders it unlikely that any new style—as distinct from idiom—will be very long-lived. But it also suggests, as does the history of European music from about 1850, that decadence may be dated from the moment when musicians start playing for critics rather than audiences, and when audiences begin looking to criticism as a guide to respectable approbation.

Much of the bop era seems, in retrospect, an orgy of sanctimonious self-indulgence and self-congratulation. The jazz musician, previously content to be a successful entertainer, and now suddenly made aware of his artistic worth by a flood of pubescent hyperbole, was ill-equipped by background, upbringing or education to deal with this ardent

141

embrace. It went to his head; and he was easily persuaded that a true Artist never gives a square an even break.

What had begun as a device to exclude the square musician at Minton's and other gathering places of the new elite was sustained in more public performance to exclude the square lay listener, too, the trick being to make a secret of the musical enterprise. Frank Tirro, in an article titled "The Silent Tradition in Jazz" in the July 1967 issue of *The Musical Quarterly,* has defined the secret as "the unperformed *cantus firmus*," meaning, of course, the more or less familiar tune which, with its chord changes, would be the musicians' point of departure, but which would be neither announced nor played. Tirro offers Charlie Parker's "Ko-Ko," derived from the chords of Ray Noble's "Cherokee," as an example of the procedure. He then goes on to show how the riddle might be wrapped in an enigma:

Almost ten years after Charlie Parker worked over "Cherokee," Warne Marsh composed "Marshmallow" to the same chord pattern. Marsh was a member of the Cool Jazz group; Parker was a member of the Hot. The pun on Marsh's own name in the title is obvious, but I do not think it too far-fetched to imagine that Marsh was paying homage to Charlie Parker by creating a cool marshmallow for Parker's hot cocoa.

Tirro concludes perceptively:

The enigmatic titles of many jazz compositions are reminiscent of Renaissance and Baroque puzzle canon instructions, anagram texts and acrostic dedications. They are all marks of a circle of initiates.

He might have added that many of the puzzles and "in" jokes were in the music itself as well as in the titles. Small wonder, then, that lay listeners who had rejoiced in the amiable forthrightness of Sidney Bechet, Louis Armstrong and Duke Ellington, of Benny Goodman and the Dorseys, or the younger enthusiasts who had danced to the lilting rhythms and silken reeds of Glenn Miller, turned away. If was as if the house band at Luther's Tavern in Nuremberg had played "The Art of the Fugue" for E. T. A. Hoffmann and his friends.

There is no harm in "The Art of the Fugue," or in making "Ko-Ko" out of "Cherokee" or "Lester Leaps In" out of "Honeysuckle Rose." There is, indeed, much good. But there is a time and a place and an audience for such exercises. Bach never intended "The Art of the Fugue" for public performance, nor the "Goldberg Variations," either. Even the preludes and fugues of "The Well-Tempered Clavier" were designed as studies for his children and as demonstrations of equal temperament. Had anyone suggested to Bach that large audiences would one day assemble for three evenings in a row to hear *all* the preludes and fugues, or sit through *all* the "Goldberg Variations" at a single session, Bach, I suspect, would have put him down as a lunatic. Nor can Beethoven have ever expected a very wide public for the last piano sonatas and string quartets. Both Bach and Beethoven knew perfectly well how to address themselves to a large lay public, and both of them did it, repeatedly and successfully. But that is not a fashionable view of the matter.

Insofar as bop musicians felt themselves to be emulating the Great Composers in assuming the creative artist's right to dictate the terms of his relationship to a paying public, they were only demonstrating again how dangerous a little knowledge can be; and they were encouraged in their delusion by a numerous coterie of jazz fans who, for a time, made of bop an "in" thing. Among them, certainly, were many who can have had only a hazy notion of what was going on, but who

143

achieved fluency in the "in" jargon readily enough and could usually disguise their bewilderment by avoiding self-incriminating questions and irrelevant observations.

For the lay listener there was, moreover, a compensating factor in the bop musician's frequently transcendental virtuosity. It may have been, in part, to redeem the esoteric character of their improvisation that bop musicians laced their melodic inventions and harmonic adventures with feats of instrumental derring-do. There was, of course, a bit of old-fashioned carving about it, too. The result, in any case, was something that a lay public could recognize and understand.

Trumpets were played higher than they had ever before been played, or ever should have been played. Saxophones were made to yield a thousand or so notes a measure, along with uncouth grunts and squeals at the extremes of the range. Double-bass players developed a dexterity beyond the wildest imagining of any symphony orchestra bassist, and drummers opened up an entirely new world of rhythmic and percussive variety. Pianists adopted a driving velocity modeled on the symptoms of Bud Powell's infatuation with Parker, although tending to play as if their left hands had just been caught in a drummer's rimshot. Vibraharp and guitar virtuosity added to the fun.

As employed by the best musicians, these technical devices and excursions, and even the recourse to the extremes of instrumental range and the defiance of traditional concepts of musical sound, served a legitimate structural and expressive purpose. This could be, under ideal circumstances, an ecstatic as well as an esoteric music. Granted an immaculate execution, there was listening pleasure even in pure instrumental athleticism.

But the fundamental requirements of such exertion are that it be exceptional and that it be perfect. In bop the resources of trumpets, trombones and saxophones were quickly exhausted, while on piano the jazz musician has never surpassed the virtuosity of the best Serious pianists. Since in virtuosity, as in athletics, what one man accomplishes will quickly be accomplished by others, the initially exceptional soon became commonplace. With less inventive musicians it also became a bore. In the past few years there has been repeated in bop the rueful history of the *castrato* singer who, at the close of the eighteenth century, disgraced himself and his music with desperate but vain exhibitions of familiar and no longer purposeful vocal acrobatics.

In terms of audience participation this has been a serious matter, since for many in the audience, possibly the majority, executive brilliance had always been the principal attraction, just as it had been for all but the connoisseurs among the opera enthusiasts of the age of *bel canto.* Bop, moreover, as distinguished from less esoteric jazz styles, had, like *opera seria,* become stereotyped in its format—a ritual sequence of solos, or choruses, including—inevitably and often intolerably—double bass and drums, sandwiched between a unison beginning and a unison ending.

To the finest of the bop musicians, instrumental virtuosity had always been incidental to the primary concern, which was the exploration of new harmonic, melodic and rhythmic escape routes from the conventions of the popular song. Their prosecution of the search might have been less punishing had they moderated the pace to accommodate what almost certainly would have been a sympathetic public, or had they let the public in on their enterprise. But this the more dogmatic refused to do; and the public, once the initially compensatory virtuosity began to pall, or the musician's virtuosity to decline, was left with a musical puzzle that few were qualified to solve or thought worth solving.

The bop musician's fundamental error, however, was neither his self-indulgent esotericism nor his incidental dependence upon virtuosity. It was his neglect of song. He disregarded the eternal and immutable factor of *memorable* melody. Here, again, he was following Serious-music fashion—and courting a comparable disaster. Nothing is so insidious in contemporary attitudes about music—and nothing so destructive—as the tendency to think of a good tune as somehow inferior, or ignominious, and to think of the man who writes one, or sings one, or plays one, as a trifler.

The Great Composers, from Bach to Bartók, knew better. They knew that without a *remembered* melody the listener is lost, and further composition futile. They sought good melodies, and, having found them, they assisted the listener's memory by repeating them. In elaborating their good melodies, and in subjecting them to juxtaposition and development, they made sure that the remembered strain was not easily lost.

Repetition is the secret, and it always has been, which accounts for the durability of the conventional AABA form favored by so many of the most successful American songwriters. It offers two repetitions of an eight-measure motive within the thirty-two measures of the tune, the repetitions separated by an eight-measure bridge, or release. Most well-remembered melodies are repetitive within themselves—the "Barcarolle" from *The Tales of Hoffmann,* for example, or Vincent Youmans's "Tea for Two," or Irving Berlin's "Say It Isn't So," or almost any melody in any Beethoven symphony.

Because musical analysis has concentrated more on what a composer did with a melody than on the melody itself, it has become fashionable to think of melody as merely incidental to elaboration and development. And in the last stages of the decadence of the European idiom, composers have abandoned melody altogether. True serial music indeed, seems designed specifically to frustrate remembrance. This is about as cockeyed a notion of composition as can readily be imagined.

The improvisations of the bop musicians, for all the concern with chordal harmony, have been melodic enough, but they have not been, as a rule, *memorably* melodic. And they have been rendered less easily memorable by denying the listener the remembered melodic nucleus. This is not to say that they have been without genius. Many improvisations have been transcribed into conventionally legible notation and exposed to detailed and flattering analysis. It is not unlikely that in years to come the improvisations of Charlie Parker, Dizzy Gillespie, Miles Davis, Charles Mingus, Thelonious Monk, Bud Powell and John Coltrane will be required study for young musicians, just as Bach fugues are required studies today.

Like Bach's fugues, bop improvisations tend to sound all alike to the uninitiated or merely casual listener. But Bach, at least, usually built his fugues on memorable themes that remain easily identifiable through all their transformations, and recur in their original form. The melodic workings of bop are more difficult for the lay listener not because they are more complex but because they offer so few obvious clues.

A good part of the trouble may be traced to the jazz musician's preoccupation with harmony. His melodic course has too often been determined by harmonic decisions, a circumstance doubly unfortunate in an age when chord progressions no longer fascinate the lay listener as they did fifty or a hundred years ago. In jazz, moreover, and especially in bop, the progressions have tended to be obscured by the rapidity with which they occur at fast tempos, not to mention the distracting and sometimes disturbing activity of the

147

drums, the often ambiguous intonation of a fast-moving bass and the casual performance of the pianist, feeding chords and thinking of other things while awaiting his turn at bat.

This concern with chromatic harmony was probably something that jazz had to go through as part of the process of achieving musical maturity within the general framework of Western music. Earlier forms of jazz had been harmonically primitive. The jazz musician of the 1940s, at last aware of his music as an integral phenomenon in the evolution of Western music, had to catch up; and instead of merely studying the European masters—although many of them did that, too— he worked it all out, and into, his own music, curiously unaware of the fact that what he was learning and discovering was precisely what the Serious composer had discarded as no longer viable.

A further liability has been a tendency to think instrumentally rather than vocally. To the modern jazz musician an instrument, any instrument, is not a vocal substitute but a horn. His predecessors, in this respect at least, were better counseled by their instincts than the younger men have been counseled by their brains. They all sang when they blew— Sidney Bechet, King Oliver, Louis Armstrong, Ben Webster, Johnny Hodges, Coleman Hawkins, Lester Young, Henry Allen, Barney Bigard, and so on. They worked over a melody. Their successors tended to work over the chord changes. And in their preoccupation with harmonic refinement and instrumental virtuosity, they forgot how to sing.

The consequence has been professional and personal disaster. Jazz musicians of the bop era accepted the Serious-music community's flattering conception of the Artist as standing above and beyond the disciplines of the marketplace, and of music as being something more than song, without first having been accepted by society as Artists. They hoped to prove that what they played was not Popular music; and in that they succeeded. But the right people were not listening. The Serious composer's penalty for his refusal, or inability, to entertain, or even to move, may be a purgatory no more hideous than a university campus. For the jazz musician it is a matter of life and death—or a change of style, both musical and social.

That the alternatives have been understood and acknowledged is evident in what has come to be known, loosely, as avant-garde, or New or Free Jazz. There are as many varieties of the New Jazz as there are individuals playing it; but they all suggest a decision on the part of young jazzmen to renounce popularity in favor of a fashionable modernity, to accept society's concession to the Artist of the right to express himself in any manner and on any terms that may suit his disposition or convenience, and to support his claim to artistic status by a music unrelated to any musical vernacular.

And their enterprise has not been without a certain grotesque success. They have, at least, got themselves talked about, even by that type of Serious musician who will take almost any music seriously that seems purposefully to defy normal musical sensibility. And Ornette Coleman, for the singular noises he makes, has been rewarded not only with a Guggenheim Foundation grant but also, in Great Britain, with official classification as a Concert Artist, thus exempting him from the regulations governing the exchange of British and American jazz musicians.

In terms of the musician's relationship with the lay public, this new freedom—or invitation to license—has produced two distinctive attitudes: studied amiability and studied defiance. On the one hand are Charles Lloyd and John Handy, walking on what Mike Hennessey, of the British weekly *Melody Maker,* has called "the sunny side of the Free Jazz street."

149

Lloyd, for example, likes to speak of his music as producing "love vibrations." This would hardly fit the sounds made by Albert Ayler and Archie Shepp, which seem to be telling the audience quite explicitly to take it or leave it.

In either case, the effect has been to stimulate public reaction, for the time being at least. Audiences find both Lloyd's eccentric amiability and Shepp's exultant intransigence preferable to the mannered indifference of many bop musicians, notably Miles Davis, who can rarely be bothered to acknowledge an audience's applause. Both Lloyd and Shepp, moreover, in their uninhibited and picturesque exhibitionism, which extends to conspicuously outlandish attire, achieve a kind of inverse showmanship. They manage, in a bizarre fashion, to be entertaining. There is, indeed, a certain delightful paradox in the fact that some of these musicians, strident in their insistence that it is not an Artist's business to entertain, have prospered precisely as entertainers, by virtue of a purposeful and defiant eccentricity.

The young avant-garde jazz musician, in his quest of self-expression, acknowledges neither harmonic nor melodic restraints. The man with a horn just blows, and when two or more players are gathered together, they may all blow at once. The drummer wants to liberate himself from the tedium of providing a steady pulse. He wants to play "melodically" and to try his hand at eccentric rhythms. And the bass player, whose Baroque-like *continuo* line had, in bop, shared both rhythmic and harmonic responsibilities with pianist and drummer, is impatient with "playing time."

This is musical anarchy, and it has been denounced as anarchy by any number of older jazz musicians, including bop musicians, just as they themselves were denounced as anarchists by the "moldy figs" of the 1940s, and as Louis Armstrong himself was denounced by the primitives when he demolished the tightly knit ensemble of New Orleans jazz. The denunciations, too, are expressed in a kind of picturesque and uninhibited language that the professional critic can only envy—and quote.

Herbie Mann, for example, on Archie Shepp in a *Down Beat* Blindfold Test: "It sounds like Eddie 'Lockjaw' Davis with a sore throat." Or the same Eddie Davis on Shepp, also in a Blindfold Test: "Please take that off—discontinue that. I have one word for that—tragedy!" Or Calvin Jackson on Ornette Coleman, in a Blindfold Test: "It sounds like a Motorola running backwards." Or Shelly Manne on Albert Ayler, in a Blindfold Test: "It's a shuck. . . . You can get the same results from sticking a microphone in the midst of all that humanity in Times Square on New Year's Eve— scream, rant, rave, blow horns, honk. . . ." Or Kenny Dorham on Ayler in the July 15, 1965 issue of *Down Beat:* "If this thing isn't quarantined, we'll all be in the garment center pushing wagons." Or "Sonny" Murray on avant-grade drummers in a *Down Beat* interview (March 23, 1967) : "They sound like a washing machine that's been left plugged in, not realizing that the laundry has been cleaned." Or Ruby Braff on the avant-garde in general in the English *Jazz Journal* (August 1965): "They sound like lunatics!"

Professional jazz criticism has been predictably more circumspect. Restraint is thrown aside occasionally, as in the coverage by Dan Morgenstern and Ira Gitler in *Down Beat* (August 10, 1967) of the Albert Ayler Quintet's appearance at the Newport Festival: "The group sounded, at times, like a Salvation Army band on LSD." But such candid and felicitous observations are rare. Anxious not to appear as reactionaries, or fearful of being left high and dry should the New Thing catch on, the jazz critics ape modern Serious-music criticism and hedge. Or they take the musicians' side against

151

the audience, as in this review by Bob Houston in *Melody Maker* (November 4, 1967) of Shepp's appearance with Jazz Expo '67 in London:

> Was it jazz? Was it Black Power? Was it all a put-on? Was it Shepp's way, as someone later remarked, of "defecating on the audience"? Whatever it was, it drove quite a few paying customers right out into the cold night, and inspired cries of "Rubbish!" and "Play some jazz!" from sections of the audience. Whatever it was, the power to move an audience, even if it is off their back sides and toward the nearest exit, is something that has been missing in jazz for far too long.

Quite a lot of modern musical history is implicit in such an observation, and similar observations could be made of the present situation in the graphic arts, the theater and literature. Recourse to shock and gimmickry, to silly eccentricity and pompous vulgarity, is the last resort of any art that has lost its capacity to make itself attractive to a paying public by more decorous means—any art, in short, that begins to sense its own impending obsolescence. The condition of jazz is not dissimilar to that of Serious music, the distinction being that the Serious-music audience, having reconciled itself to aural assault as a tariff on Beethoven and Brahms, is rather beyond shock. For shock, following an initial reaction of indignation or excitement, is easily absorbed. Immunity follows, and then boredom, as Ralph Gleason pointed out in the *New York Post* on March 25, 1967:

> When tenor saxophonists get up there and blow for what seems like an hour, followed by a trumpet player who does the same thing, it doesn't matter that they have technical command of their instruments. What matters is that they do not get to the point. On records, the outpouring of long improvisations by

any clown capable of conning somebody into a recording session simply is not art. What's needed in jazz is a lot less freedom and a lot more editing. Freedom to create, but not freedom to bore.

Gleason was too tactful, probably, to suggest that more careful editing of critics' copy in the jazz magazines might have prompted better editing of records and public performances, and helped to head off the present debacle. Jazz critics are as bewildered as anybody else by what is going on in jazz today, and they do not, as a rule, like what they hear. But a considerable portion of the blame must fall upon them. In their innocent eagerness to see jazz established as an art form, they encouraged musicians in the cultivation of highfalutin attitudes and highbrow posturing, applauding their divorce from the mass audience and censuring as apostasy every commercial deviation and every "concession" to popular taste.

The fruit of the critics' evangelism was apparent, in the work of the second bop generation, in the playing of such superlative instrumentalists as Sonny Rollins, John Coltrane and Eric Dolphy, and it ripened in the work of the conspicuously less accomplished plastic saxophone utterances of Ornette Coleman, from whose arrival in New York in 1959 the avant-garde phase is customarily dated. Some of the more perceptive critics began to have doubts, and some of the older musicians, too. "Is that what the critics are digging?" asked Miles Davis after listening to a record by pianist Cecil Taylor on a *Down Beat* Blindfold Test. "If there ain't nothing to listen to, they might just as well admit it."

But it was too late. As with the Serious-music critics who had climbed onto the post-Webern serialist bandwagon at the end of the last war—especially the German and British critics —and who suddenly found themselves confronted with the annual ritual horrors of Donaueschingen and Darmstadt, there was no turning back. Prisoners of their own commitment and momentum, they could challenge a detail here or there, but they could not acknowledge fundamental error.

Nor could they go into opposition without playing into the hands of the adversary, without creating precisely the kind of controversy upon which the avant-garde feeds. Nothing succeeds like scandal in this esthetically decadent age; and it would sometimes seem that only scandal succeeds. A unanimous sounding of the alarm, a coordinated denunciation, might just conceivably have had a salutary effect, both in Serious music and in jazz. But there will never be unanimity among critics, even assuming a near unanimity of opinion. Some will always seek to distinguish themselves as heralds of progress, and a majority will prefer cautious equivocation to candor. And so there has been just enough denunciation to kindle the essential controversy but not enough to be decisive—or to lend effective support to the numerous musicians who have preferred candor to equivocation.

The young musicians of the avant-garde have known perfectly well that controversy is their only dependable stock-in-trade; and they have sensed instinctively, if they did not determine it wittingly, that jazz had reached a stage—arrived at in Serious music fifty years ago—where anything goes; that critical timidity had contributed to a state of affairs where nothing was any longer demonstrably bad. All the musician had to say was "That's the way I hear it" or "That's the way I feel it." And that was that.

There is no sure way of distinguishing between sincerity and opportunism in such matters, or between original genius and charlatanism. The problem for the true professional is that the oddball gets the headlines whether he be charlatan or genius or, as happens sometimes, a bit of each. Pertinent in this respect is a rueful observation by Eddie "Lockjaw"

Davis, appended to his remarks on Archie Shepp quoted above: "It's just a tragedy that he's chosen such an erratic trail to success; but who knows, he may be recognized through just such a revolt."

Drummer Roy Haynes, in an interview with LeRoi Jones in *Down Beat,* in the issue of March 29, 1962, described more precisely the predicament of the unflamboyant professional: "I bet if I was some kind of nut or something, you know, weird or a junkie or something, I'd get a lot of notice. But there doesn't seem to be too much attention paid to guys who make a normal scene. I mean, guys who make all their gigs and raise families. It's a wild thing."

Leonard Feather, always one of the clearest heads among the jazz critical fraternity, has said: "The self-conscious attempt to become controversial is one of the most prevalent and obnoxious forms of would-be popularization." And musicians themselves provide the evidence. Many of them, said drummer Roy Brooks in *Down Beat* on August 10, 1967, "use avant-garde music as a bandwagon to ride to appease [*sic*] the critics."

Probably it had to happen. The young jazz musician of 1955–60 was faced with problems very similar to those that had driven Serious composers into neoclassicism or dodecaphony shortly after the turn of the century. No further progress was possible in the direction in which he had been headed without violating his traditional harmonic and melodic frame of reference. And for the same reason. He had run out of chords and things to do with them; and the public was running out of interest in the chords he played. Also, like the Serious musician, he had run out of interesting things to do on his instruments. The outer limits of virtuosity had been reached. And the instruments themselves could be made to yield no more.

But there were important differences in the respective

alternatives. The Serious composer, with a three-hundred-year tradition behind him, could look backward as a neoclassicist; or he could plunge forward into atonality, even at the risk of alienating his audience. The jazz musician's past was still too recent to support neoclassical exercises comparable to those of Stravinsky, Prokofiev and Bartók. And his musical nature was too closely identified with intelligible, if not necessarily *memorable,* melody to accept a systematized atonality.

The jazz equivalent of neoclassicism would have been a blending of New Orleans or swing with the devices of modern jazz; but something very close to such a blend had been attained in the bands of Duke Ellington, Count Basie and Woody Herman, and in the middle-of-the-road styles identified with Earl Hines, Erroll Garner, Oscar Peterson, Dave Brubeck and Stan Getz. Nor could he go back beyond swing and New Orleans to the blues. A blues revival was well under way, with the Mississippi Delta and the Southwest yielding ancient but still audible singers who could produce the real thing. And the middle ground between blues and jazz had long ago been preempted by gospel song and rhythm-and-blues, by country-and-western and rock 'n' roll. The modern jazz musician was neither disposed nor able to compete with Memphis Slim and T-Bone Walker, or with Ray Charles and B.B. King. In divorcing himself from the mass public, he had deserted the mainstream of American music, and the mainstream had flowed on without him.

There was always, of course, the lure of Serious music, with its beguiling aura of respectability; and many jazz musicians, beginning with Jelly Roll Morton and Duke Ellington, have looked in that direction for a passageway into the future, unaware, apparently, that Serious music had only a past, and that some Serious composers were even looking to jazz for an exit from Serious music's own dead end. Outstanding among many thoughtful jazz musicians who have succumbed, at one time or another, to this flirtation have been Stan Kenton, William Russo, George Russell, Teddy Charles, Teo Macero, Gil Evans, John Lewis, Jimmy Giuffre and Johnny Dankworth.

The lesson to be drawn from their experience would seem to be that, while it is possible for a musician to be conversant with both idioms, little may be hoped for from any kind of studied blending, least of all from blending with the sterile devices of serialism. The jazz composer too often ends by writing Serious music for a jazz band, and the result, as Whitney Balliett noted in *The New Yorker* a decade ago (September 13, 1958), is "preciousness, musical tricks, the stifling of spontaneity, pure dullness, an over-attention to form, and a general solemnity and self-consciousness. It has often seemed," Balliett concluded, "as if jazz—so graceful, surprising and elusive at its best—might eventually evaporate, like a restless hired man."

The young jazz musician, therefore, had only two alternatives: to swim with the mainstream of American music, which had already absorbed a succession of earlier jazz styles, or to forge ahead. The former posed no idiomatic incompatibility. Most Popular music, in the vocabulary of any but the self-conscious jazzman, or jazz critic, was jazz, or had a lot of jazz in it, particularly in up-tempo performance. Many excellent jazz musicians chose this alternative. They moved into the studios, and many of them prospered, both as executant musicians and as composer-arrangers.

But this choice seemed to imply a renunciation of the jazz musician's identity as an Artist, a sacrifice of status, even if the status were acknowledged only by the musician's own peers and critics. There was the stigma of "going commercial," or "selling out." And there were other problems. Studio work demanded the acceptance of studio discipline and the satisfaction of studio technical requirements and, specifically, of studio reading requirements. Many gifted young jazz musicians were either unwilling or unable to meet these conditions; and there was felt to be an additional inhibition in the alleged discrimination against black musicians by the studios. Through choice, or through want of choice, they "stayed with jazz" and endeavored to secure for it a more fashionable future.

The young jazz musician's recent performance suggests a frustrated neoclassical yearning. Unable to be specifically reminiscent, he has tended to invoke the past as an endorsement of his forward progress, rationalizing his radical course as an extension of the spirit and inflections of the blues. This path had been indicated to him at the height of the bop era by a bop derivative called "soul music" and by a manner of playing called "funky," a reaction, obviously, to the increasingly intellectual flavor of bop. Prominently identified with "soul" were Charles Mingus, John Coltrane, Sonny Rollins, Eric Dolphy, Cannonball Adderley, Les McCann, Horace Silver and Jimmy Smith.

The attractive feature of the blues was, for them, not the rudimentary harmonic formulas nor the primitive imagery of the lyrics but the ecstatic utterance of voice and guitar, the uninhibited emotional outpouring, even more conspicuously characteristic, perhaps, of gospel song, which, for many jazz musicians, was still a vivid childhood memory. As David Kennard, writing in the June 1967 issue of *Jazz Journal*, has put it, the avant-garde "has shown up what has been missing in so much modern jazz: the vocal quality. It has restored to jazz the beautiful capacity of a musical instrument to sound like, or remind one of, a human voice talking, moaning, singing, shouting; expressing human emotions and feelings."

Other professional critics have made similar observations. Don Heckman, writing of Eric Dolphy in *Down Beat*, has noted "scream-like glissandos, crisply articulated speech passages and blinding bursts of smeared notes," as well as "a savage quality that recalled music of a much earlier era." Leonard Feather, as long ago as 1957, heard in Mingus's music "an attempt to return blues-shouting elements to instrumental music." And Mort Maizlish has said of Archie Shepp: "He often plays with a rough, brutal attack, reflecting both jazz origins and the sounds of the street, of rhythm-and-blues and of Negro folk tunes and chants."

All of which reads better than most of the music sounds. It is putting the best of all possible faces on a kind of music that is often ugly and obstreperously self-indulgent, betraying the attitude disclosed to *Melody Maker* in the fall of 1966 by alto saxophonist Charlie Mariano: "I don't want to hear pleasant music today. I want to hear screaming and hollering and kicking and biting. That's what the world's about today. And I believe the music should reflect life. Life is a bit chaotic, and I think jazzmen should express something of the way life is lived."

Many Serious composers and their spokesmen have taken a similar position to rationalize the tortured structures and barnyard sounds of "advanced" Serious music, as if music had no more edifying function than to duplicate and compound the disorders of everyday life. Mariano's recipe sounds about as artistic as a temper tantrum, and so does a good deal of avant-garde jazz, just as a more amiable variety of avant-garde jazz can sometimes come pretty close to infant prattle. "A baby," said Coleman Hawkins to *Melody Maker* (September 16, 1967), "can make noises like that."

Infantilism is, indeed, the most distressing aspect of the New Jazz—puerile attitudes and puerile expression. The elements of this music are variously described by its makers as "feeling," "energy," "tension," etc. The young bassist Charlie Haden, in a *Down Beat* interview (March 9, 1967), told how Ornette Coleman, in 1958, "wasn't playing on the chord changes. . . . He was playing off the *feeling*." And David C. Hunt, describing the music of Coleman, Archie Shepp, Don Cherry, Bill Dixon and others in the July 1967 issue of *Jazz*, spoke of "animalistic chaos representing a high degree of raw ego expression. It is quite clear," he added, "that the jazz artist who chooses to project himself through strict musical values, as opposed to a personal expression haphazardly injected with bits of musical reference, travels a more difficult road to recognition."

The obvious parallel to this kind of "raw ego expression" is the child rambling along in its own language before it has learned to express its thoughts and feeling in language and gestures intelligible and acceptable to the community into which it was born. There are many references in the critical and descriptive literature of modern jazz to musicians "talking" to each other in their music, which suggests infant brothers conversing in a language unintelligible to their parents. There is nothing wrong in all this, but nothing especially admirable, either—or anything sufficiently remarkable to make it worth a price of admission.

For most professional musicians, probably, one of the memorable episodes of musical education has been the discovery, as a performer, that the listener—teacher, critic or friend—has not heard what the student heard in his own performance. The student knows what he *intends* to play, and his perception of what he actually plays is influenced by the preconceived image. It is a mark of the true professional that he knows how he sounds *to others,* that he knows how others hear him. This is an essential element of knowledge for any performing artist; for the audience is moved by what it *hears,* not by eloquent sounds that may exist only in the artist's imagination, and it rewards the artist accordingly.

Command of the principles and techniques of communication is what art is all about. The avant-garde jazz musician—and, often enough, the avant-garde Serious composer, too—disregards this ultimately simple proposition, insofar as he understands it at all; and he insists on his right to speak a language of his own, or a language intelligible only to one or more sympathetic colleagues. What he means by Free Jazz, in other words, is independence from the responsibility of channeling his feelings—presumably genuine and intense—into the forms by which these feelings, sensations, sentiments, perceptions of the beautiful, and so on, can be communicated to others.

In this sense the frustrated neoclassicist becomes an uninhibited neo-atavist. There may be a good deal of instrumental dexterity in what he does, and there may even be talent; but there is not much art. What the young jazz musician conceives as moving forward into freedom is, in fact, a retreat into the undisciplined fantasies of the playpen and the rumpus room. And that sort of thing can become very tiresome. As an English critic wrote in *Melody Maker* of Archie Shepp's performance in Berlin, following the London workout noted earlier: "He neither had me leaping in my seat nor leaving. He just bored the pants off me."

Which tells a lot about why musicians have had less luck than graphic artists and novelists in palming off the fruits of their freedom as works of genius. One can walk away from a painting on the pretext of moving to the next, or throw a book into the trash basket in one's own home; but there is no escaping bad music, in public at least, without being publicly rude. In the normal course of events, the listener sticks it out, observes the proprieties by applauding at the end, leaves, and does not come back.

Things could be worse. The New Jazz is not, like new

Serious music, *anti*-musical or *non*-musical. It is simply primeval, embryonic. It goes back to the very beginning, which may not be a bad idea. All that it needs is organization in conformity with the expectations of a lay public. Unless, of course, the musician merely wants to play for his own edification, as he has every right to do—but then he should choose another profession. He has no call on anyone, in that case, to lend an ear—or a dollar.

As a professional musician he must sing for his supper, as professional musicians have always done. How well he eats will depend, as it has always depended, upon what he sings, for whom he sings, and how well—and it will depend upon *how well he pleases.*

The S(w)ingers

Many in the jazz community say that jazz is dead—maimed by bop, then finished off, inelegantly, by the New Jazz. Just as many, probably more, insist that jazz is very much alive. Both, I think, are right. It all depends upon what you call jazz.

There have been previous obituaries. Some jazz musicians, jazz critics and lay jazz enthusiasts felt that jazz died with New Orleans and Dixieland, others that it died with swing, just as today's mourners feel that it died with bop. The confusion arises from the fact—I, at least, propose it as a fact—that jazz is neither a new kind of music nor even a specific way of playing. It is an ugly four-letter word, of inscrutable etymology, an unfortunate and musically meaningless term that has survived a succession of musical styles of Afro-American origin—New Orleans, Dixieland, swing, bop, progressive, cool, soul—having been applied, as a symbol of idiomatic continuity and distinction, to each new style as the previous style was absorbed into the mainstream of American music. That it has not been applied to rock, the latest of the Afro-American styles, may indicate that *jazz*, as a term, is, at long last, either dead or dying. I, for one, hope so. It has never been worthy of the best music with which it has been associated.

I have suggested in an earlier chapter that *jazz* has been employed consistently as a substitute for *good* to distinguish an Afro-American original from its Euro-American dilution. This was certainly true of the period between 1940 and 1955, now referred to commonly as the Age of the Singer, in Popular music, the period dominated by Harry Belafonte, Tony Bennett, Nat King Cole, Perry Como, Bing Crosby, Billy Eckstine, Eddie Fisher, Dick Haymes, Frank Sinatra, Mel Torme, June Christy, Rosemary Clooney, Chris Connor, Doris Day, Ella Fitzgerald, Billie Holiday, Lena Horne, Kitty Kallen, Peggy Lee, Anita O'Day, Patti Page, Dinah Shore, Jo Stafford, Kay Starr, Sarah Vaughan, Dinah Washington and many, many more.

The jazz community has always been ambivalent in its view of these singers, and particularly in its view of those whom it most admires—Crosby, Sinatra, Fitzgerald, Holiday, O'Day, Torme, and Vaughan. The jazz musician's appreciation of them is disturbed by their tendency to move toward or away from the Afro-American idiom depending upon their material and their target audience; and it has been soured by the best singers' enormous commercial success, which, if associated with jazz, would compromise the jazz musician's hope of acceptance as an Artist.

This ambivalence is nowhere more evident than in the annual readers' and critics' polls in the jazz magazines, which divide the singers into two categories—Jazz and Popular—and which end, invariably, with at least half a dozen singers ranking high in both. The jazz musician and the jazz critic rationalize this inconsistency by saying that the categorization depends upon what the singer is singing, or has sung, and under what circumstances. A Sinatra, for instance, or a Tony Bennett, will appear under Jazz thanks to collaboration with Count Basie, and under Popular as the fashioner of ballads backed by Nelson Riddle. Joe Williams, conversely, a jazz singer when he was vocalist with Count Basie, became a Popular singer when songs that he had sung with Basie became popular hits. But no two critics would agree on just where the line is to be drawn.

Very few, probably, would go so far as Ralph Gleason, who has said of Crosby and Sinatra that they have the rhythmic feeling for jazz and the gift of free melodic articulation that is the essence of jazz. "Bing," he wrote in a review of Crosby's autobiographical *Call Me Lucky* (1953), "is the personification of the whole jazz movement—the relaxed, casual, natural and uninhibited approach to art." This comes too close to identifying jazz with Popular music; for few singers have been so popular as Crosby, and none, probably, with the exception of Sinatra, has so influenced Popular singing styles.

Most critics simply flounder, none more haplessly and hopelessly than Leonard Feather, who, both as encyclopedist and as editor of the *Down Beat* Blindfold Test, has had to explain or rationalize his editorial nod to this or that Popular singer. In the 1955 edition of his *Encyclopedia of Jazz,* for instance, we are told that Sinatra is "not basically a jazz performer, though his associations include occasional record dates featuring jazz musicians." In the edition of 1967, however, we learn that Sinatra, "winner of innumerable jazz [*sic*] polls, . . . strengthened his jazz association in the 60s through frequent night club appearances backed by the Count Basie Band." There is no suggestion here of any change in Sinatra's singing. It is merely that he would seem to have been keeping better company.

Of Bing Crosby we read, in the 1955 edition: "Not a jazz artist, but has been associated with jazzmen from time to time," and of Lena Horne: "mainly a popular rather than a jazz singer." Neither Crosby nor Horne is included in the edition of 1967. Nat King Cole, about whose qualifications as a jazz pianist there was never any doubt, was treated similarly: "His piano became subjugated more and more to his singing, and in the early 1950s he was a national figure in the popular scene, his jazz associations almost forgotten." And yet, in the next paragraph: "His was the first great jazz-grounded male voice since Louis Armstrong's to earn a worldwide acceptance." Nor had there been a change of heart by 1967: "though the tonal quality of Cole's voice lent a jazz character to some of his up-tempo songs, Cole, in the later years, was essentially a popular music figure."

Feather must have had qualms about including Andy Williams in a Blindfold Test (January 11, 1968) ; and the rationale employed in the editorial introduction offered yet another instructive example of the jazz community's confusion and ambivalence about singers:

Andy Williams is not a jazz singer (though Joe Williams, among others, has credited him with a jazz feeling). He is not a rock 'n' roll singer. In other words, he subscribes to neither of the two idioms now covered by *Down Beat*. Why, then, an Andy Williams Blindfold Test? First and foremost, categories aside, Andy Williams is an exceptionally *good* singer. He belongs in that middle ground that encompasses everyone from Barbra Streisand to Belafonte and from Buddy Greco to Joan Baez and all the dozens of other good singers whose names, because they are neither jazz nor rock artists, are rarely seen in these pages. Second, in the course of gathering material for a recent *Billboard* project dealing with Andy Williams, I found that he and Quincy Jones are mutual admirers (in 1960, Andy went to Paris to record with Quincy's band) ; and that numerous other jazzmen dig him, and he them.

166

Such tortuous and tortured waffling reflects, of course, the view, fashionable among jazz musicians and jazz critics, that jazz cannot be sung, that jazz is essentially an instrumentalist's art. And this view, in turn, reflects, and goes far to explain, the jazz community's failure to identify satisfactorily and come to terms with the essential and distinctive characteristics of its own music. For the art of the jazz musician, in my view, is an instrumental extension and sublimation of a musical idiom that, in its melodic, if not in its rhythmic, characteristics, is fundamentally vocal.

I have remarked earlier that the songs of the American song writer, themselves reflecting the influence of ragtime, early jazz and swing, have provided the jazz musician with his most congenial melodic materials; and I would add now only the suggestion that the art of the jazz musician, and specifically his distinctive and characteristic manner of phrasing—the shaping of the phrase around the *explicit* beat to produce a swinging momentum and a metrical freedom foreign to the European-oriented musician's rhythmic procedure—is essentially an extension of the art of the blues singer. It is so close to the Negro's wondrously musical speech that words are sensed when they are not articulated.

The Negro, as Charles Keil has pointed out so perceptively in his *Urban Blues* (1966), is a talker rather than a writer, revering oral rather than literary tradition. His music, even his instrumental music, is an extension of oratory; and those characteristics of phrase that strike the European-educated ear as exotic, and even offensive, all serve to give his playing a rhetorically articulate flavor.

Louis Armstrong is often said to sing the way he plays, but it would be more accurate, I think, to say that he plays the way he sings, that his trumpet is an instrumental extension of his voice. And it is evidence of the jazz musician's instinctive feeling for his music as a sublimation of song that Lester

167

Young, one of the most eloquent of saxophonists, could say that before improvising on any song, he first memorized the words.

This has been less true of the jazz instrumentalist since jazz moved into its bop phase, causing older, "eloquent" musicians to be downgraded in favor of younger men, more dexterous on their instruments and more sophisticated harmonically, but less musical in the singer's sense, than their elders. That the jazz community now dissociates itself from the Popular singer illustrates, in my opinion, how far jazz has moved from its own roots. For the art of the best Popular singers is itself rooted in jazz.

What many jazz musicians and jazz critics overlook—or choose to forget—is the fact that those who made the post-swing era the Age of the Singer in Popular music—while jazz was moving from swing into bop and from Popular into Art—were, almost without exception, singers who had learned their craft as vocalists with the jazz bands of the swing era: Fitzgerald, Vaughan, Holiday, Sinatra, Lee, Stafford, Shore, Starr, Horne, O'Day, Como, Christy, Connor, Clooney, Eckstine, Haymes and even Bing Crosby, whose apprenticeship was served with the bands of Paul Whiteman and Gus Arnheim.

George Simon, in his *The Big Bands* (1967), offers persuasive evidence from the singers themselves of what this experience contributed to their development as vocal artists and public performers. Sinatra, for instance, tells us in a foreword: "My greatest teacher was not a vocal coach, not the work of other singers, but the way Tommy Dorsey breathed and phrased on the trombone." Doris Day is quoted by Simon: "Being a band singer teaches you not only how to work in front of people, but also how to work with them." And Peggy Lee: "Band singing taught us the importance of

interplay with musicians. We had to work close to the arrangement. . . . I learned more about music from the men I
worked with in bands than I've learned anywhere else. They
taught me discipline and the value of rehearsing and how to
train."

The musicality—and, often enough, the musicianship—of
the best Popular singers of the midcentury must be apparent
to anyone who has heard them work in a room or who has
listened to their records, particularly the records made after
they had left the bands and struck out on their own, when
they could choose their own songs and exert a decisive influence on the character and even the personnel of the instrumental backing. It was only after leaving the bands that they
could show how fine was their instinctive musicality and how
creative they could be in the reworking and reshaping of
familiar and sometimes inferior material.

In this they profited, of course, from their experience with
the bands, including much unpleasant and exasperating experience. Living and traveling day by day, month after
month, with instrumentalists, they could not help, as Peggy
Lee says, learning a great deal about instruments and instrumentation, about tempo and instrumental phrasing, and
about the kind of backing that suited—or did not suit—both
song and singer. With them on these tours were the sidemen-
arrangers, learning the same lessons in the same tough school
of trial, error and frustration, who would later make a high
art of the instrumental backing.

As Simon describes it, speaking of the male vocalists:

. . . no matter how good a singer might be, if his leader didn't
set him up properly, either through poor planning, or because
of jealousy, his chances for success were negligible. Numerous
circumstances, over none of which vocalists exercised much con-

trol, determined how well a singer sounded, and thus ultimately how successful he could become. Some singers were forced to stray and strain outside their vocal range because an arranger happened to goof, or because they were saddled with arrangements inherited from differently pitched predecessors. Tempos, too, could hinder a vocalist. . . . On recordings, singers often appeared to disadvantage because tunes were tossed at them at the last minute. . . .

And so on. Small wonder, then, that Sinatra, recalling what he had learned from his trials as well as from his triumphs with Tommy Dorsey, could say: "If I were starting to sing all over again, I'd get a job with a band."

The decline of the big band—and, implicitly, the end of the swing era—is conveniently and conventionally dated from December 1946, when, within a period of a few weeks, eight of the most prominent bands broke up. Ignored is the extent to which the swing era lived on in those areas of musical production that the jazz musician, henceforward, would dismiss as "commercial" or "popular" and therefore "not jazz." Many of the most accomplished instrumentalists went on into bop, playing with the smaller groups, or combos, that succeeded the big bands as the music moved from the dance halls and theaters into the jazz clubs and musical bars. But many more, including many arrangers, went into the recording studios, to continue there the old association with the singers but now under circumstances far more favorable to the latter, with the singer and his record producer rather than the bandleader calling the tune and the style. Many fine musicians, too, went with the singers into the nightclubs on the road.

Released from the swing band's requirement that its music also be danceable, the singers, their arrangers and their record producers had a larger range of purpose and a new stylistic latitude. They brought to whatever they did a bit of the jazz musician's conception of phrase, although the degree differed from singer to singer and from song to song. In ballads particularly, their use of strings seemed a throwback to European conventions and to a European tradition of clinging sentimentality. But even behind the often mushy cushion of strings, there is usually audible, on the records of the time, the *continuo* prodding of a plucked bass and the insinuating momentum of a drummer's brushes and muted cymbals. In the up-tempo numbers everyone is off and swinging, and Europe is far away.

Except that in midcentury Europe—and in Japan and Australia, too—the sounds were the same. There was an enormous foreign audience for jazz, from New Orleans and Dixieland to Parker, Gillespie and Miles Davis; but in Popular music the Age of the Singer was duplicated in Europe and just about everywhere else, with native singers doing the American songs—and their own songs, too—in an American manner, and with native arrangers and instrumentalists providing backings modeled on Nelson Riddle, Gordon Jenkins, Billy May, Marty Paich and Henry Mancini. Swing did not die. It simply became so pervasive a part of the musical vernacular that the jazz musician, in his quest of distinction—and in his consciousness of jazz as an art music, separate and distinct from Popular music—disowned it.

One can say of this era, in retrospect, that there was, at least, a generally satisfactory musical spread, with something for everyone. The war generation took to bop and its many derivatives and variants, and jazz flourished. For those of less musically intellectual and exclusive disposition, there were the singers, with echoes of swing lingering in the backings. Music for dancing was penetrated agreeably by Latin-American rhythms and instrumentation. And then, suddenly, there were Joe Turner and Elvis Presley singing "Shake, Rattle and Roll," and Chubby Checker and Bill Haley's Comets.

Rock had arrived, and with it a new phase in the evolution of American music.

Rock and Pop

It was plain by the early 1960s that rock—disregarded, at first, as a passing teen-age craze—was, in fact, a musical revolution of imposing dimensions and implications, comparable, in its impact upon the middle-class, white musical community, to jazz in the mid-1920s, to swing a decade later, and to the young Sinatra a decade after that. And it proved to be just as internationally contagious. By the mid-1960s, a young Czech would be telling his American interviewer, "Rock is to us what jazz was to our parents."

Rock represented, as both early jazz and swing had done, a fusion of black and white, with black again the vital, new creative source. But whereas jazz had proceeded from a collision of Africa and Europe in urban America, rock was an American blend of urban and rural black and rural white. The diverse elements of which it was compounded had long been familiar to millions of Americans, black and white, in two indigenous styles known respectively as country-and-western and rhythm-and-blues. But not until both country-and-western and rhythm-and-blues broke their traditional subcultural and regional barriers had either of them exerted any considerable influence on the musical taste of the nation as a whole.

Country-and-western originated in the ballads and the dances of rural America, primarily in the isolated mountain areas of the South. These ballads and dances, in turn, were rooted in, and initially hardly distinguishable from, the ballads and dances that the early settlers had brought with them from the British Isles and from Europe. The history of country-and-western music, insofar as its future impact on American music as a whole is concerned, begins with its dissemination outside the immediate family group and community, first by the phonograph record and then by radio. Robert Shelton, folk and country music critic of *The New York Times,* in his book, *The Country Music Story* (1966), dates this dissemination from the recording by Okeh of Fiddling John Carson in Atlanta on June 14, 1923.

It may be dated more appropriately, as Shelton points out, from the six years between 1927 and 1933 when records made by Jimmie Rodgers, the "Singing Brakeman," sold twenty million copies. Rodgers died of tuberculosis in 1933, at the age of thirty-five; but when he was elected to the Country Music Association's Hall of Fame in 1961, the citation identified him as "the man who started it all." After him came the Carter Family, Hank Williams, Roy Acuff, Hank Snow, Eddy Arnold, Tennessee Ernie Ford and literally hundreds of others extending to Chet Atkins, Johnny Cash, Roger Miller and Buck Owens today.

The most fateful date of all, probably, is November 28, 1925, when Station WSM in Nashville broadcast a program called *Barn Dance,* the first of a series of Saturday night broadcasts, known since 1927 as *Grand Ole Opry.* It is the longest continuous radio program ever presented in the

United States. *Grand Ole Opry* has made Nashville the center of country music.

The weekly broadcast from the Ryman Auditorium, now known as the Grand Ole Opry House, is attended by audiences of upwards of 5,000. Its listening audience is estimated at 10,000,000. The total American audience for country-and-western is thought to be on the order of 35,000,000; and this audience is also served by more than 2,200 radio stations in the United States and Canada, of which number, according to Shelton, 210 present country music exclusively. As of 1963, some 131 television stations were also broadcasting country music regularly.

The evolution of rhythm-and-blues offers no such handy guideposts, although it is pertinent to note that Ralph Peer, the Okeh records scout who had recorded Fiddling John Carson in 1923, went on from Atlanta to Kansas City, where he heard a small three-piece combo led by Bennie Moten, later to become the most influential figure in the development of a Kansas City big-band style ultimately perfected by Count Basie. Peer took Moten to St. Louis and recorded the combo there in the fall of the same year. Peer's interests were commercial rather than musicological; but the coincidence of these two recording dates reflects the proximity of white country music and black country blues, an acknowledgment of which is essential to the identification and assessment of the principal sources of the American mainstream.

Although what is known commonly as country blues has been researched exhaustively and well, there had not been, until the publication of Charles Keil's *Urban Blues* in 1966, any adequate investigation of more recent developments. Keil himself attributes this to a "moldy fig" mentality among the researchers, mostly white, comparable to that of the early jazz enthusiasts who felt that "real" jazz ended with Sidney

175

Bechet, King Oliver and Louis Armstrong. And he gives an amusing caricature of the criteria against which a typical researcher measures a performer's eligibility as an exponent of the "real" blues:

Old age: the performer should preferably be more than sixty years old, blind, arthritic and toothless. Obscurity: the blues singer should not have performed in public or have made a recording in at least twenty years; among deceased bluesmen, the best seem to be those who appeared in a big city one day in the 1920s, made four to six recordings, and then disappeared into the countryside forever. Correct tutelage: the singer should have played with, or been taught by, some legendary figure. Agrarian milieu: a bluesman should have lived the bulk of his life as a sharecropper, coaxing mules and picking cotton, uncontaminated by city influences.

Keil recognizes the romantic appeal of this type of archeology, and he concedes its musicological value. But he is probably right in discerning an element of escapism in it, too:

By concentrating on old-timers and scoring today's blues as commercial and decadent, the writer can effectively avert his eyes from the urban ghetto conditions that spawn the contemporary forms. . . . It is so much easier to reminisce with old bluesmen, collect rare records and write histories than it is properly to assess a career-conscious singer, analyze an on-going blues scene and attempt to understand the blues as a Chicago Negro in 1966 understands them.

And he is right, too, about the balm of antiquity: "A coarse lyric of thirty years ago has poetic qualities and historical interest; much the same kind of lyric of today is considered frivolous and not worthy of scholarly attention."

176

Which could be said of the scholar's approach to Popular music in general. Popular music seems to become fit for Serious attention only when it is old enough to be classified as folk music. Keil comes close to the scholar's Achilles heel when he quotes Big Bill Broonzy: "I guess all songs is folk songs. I never heard no horse sing 'em."

Plotting the course of the blues from the fields of the South and Southwest to the urban ghettos of the North is not easy, and least of all for that period in the 1920s and 1930s when, in Kansas City and other centers of the Midwest and Southwest, blues and jazz were, in Keil's words, "so tightly fused that the musicians themselves usually made no distinction between them." To the world at large, thanks to the "moldy fig" researchers, the blues suggests an aging Negro with a guitar, singing a twelve-measure strain in the classic AAB form. But the blues singers of Kansas City, in the 1920s and 1930s, were singing to the accompaniment, and to the responses of, other instruments—saxophones, drums, double bass, guitar and piano.

It sounded like early Count Basie; and that is just about what it was. This is a decisive fact of American musical history; for out of that conjunction of jazz and blues came not only Jimmy Rushing, Joe Turner and Walter Brown, forerunners of today's urban blues singers, but also Jimmie Lunceford, Count Basie, Ben Webster, Jo Jones, Hot Lips Page, Lester Young, Charlie Parker, Charlie Christian and other influential jazz musicians, some of whom would be among the founding fathers of bop.

When jazz and blues parted company categorically—a convenient date is 1938, when the fall of the Pendergast regime ended the musical prosperity of Kansas City—blues continued to evolve as a music by, of, for and about urban blacks, with activity and production centered in Memphis and Chicago, while jazz, centered in New York and later also on the West Coast, was directed primarily at an audience of white intellectuals and evolved as a music in which white and black musicians, as well as white and black listeners, could participate on equal terms.

The larger middle-class, urban white community remained, throughout an entire generation, largely ignorant of all that had happened, and was still happening, in the blues— and in country music, too. When it heard something close to the real thing, in the collaboration of Jimmy Rushing, Joe Williams and Joe Turner with Count Basie, for instance, it thought of this as jazz. The more knowledgeable among the whites, *i.e.*, those who followed jazz, were vaguely aware of a music known in the trade as rhythm-and-blues, the term stemming from the new blues singer's use of a rhythm section. Many were aware, too, that a number of black jazz musicians had "graduated" from rhythm-and-blues to jazz. Ignorance and indifference were probably encouraged by the black jazz musician's own tendency to regard rhythm-and-blues condescendingly as a vulgar style, inferior to jazz, the latter now to be thought of as the art form of American music.

Louis Jordan, one of the most influential personalities in the evolution of the urban blues, has described the separation of jazz from the blues in these terms: "Those guys [the jazz musicians] really wanted to play mostly for themselves, and I wanted to play for people." Those who want to play for people must be prepared to accept popular judgment, and to adapt themselves to popular taste. The urban blues was shaped by the tastes of the new urban black masses.

Acceptance of the urban blues by the white listener requires a fundamental and far-reaching readjustment of musical criteria. The heavy, rocking, driving beat, the assertive clanging of the electric guitars, the screeching saxophones, the singers' constant employment of an ecstatic head voice, and a decibel count maintained at the limit of aural tolerance —all these come as a shock to those brought up on Beethoven, Wagner and Verdi, or Bing Crosby, Frank Sinatra and Peggy Lee, or even on Dizzy Gillespie, Charlie Parker and Miles Davis. Compared even to the later phases of bop, it is rough stuff. The closest thing to it, in the average white listener's acquaintance, is gospel song; but since gospel song is known to white listeners largely through the relatively decorous recordings of such singers as Mahalia Jackson, rather than through actual experience of the real thing in fundamentalist churches, it is not an entirely adequate preparation.

But it is this music, rather than jazz, that has nourished the mainstream of Western musical evolution in the past fifteen years. Not that B.B. King, Bobby Bland and Jr. Parker have become the new Bing Crosbys and Frank Sinatras, or even the Nat King Coles, Ella Fitzgeralds, Lena Hornes and Harry Belafontes. As formerly with jazz, there has been dilution, accommodation and adaptation. The white community has appropriated the new and essential characteristics and bent them to its own requirements. These are not, to be sure, the requirements of the older white generation, for whom the adjustment, even with dilution, is too great. But the younger whites have heard in this music a reflection of their own loneliness and defiance and emancipative urge, and they have made it—or something like it—a music of their own.

The key figure in opening this music to a young white mass audience was Elvis Presley, a country singer. As Shelton describes it:

Presley's mixture of country songs with a strong beat of Negro rhythm and blues formed a new style called rockabilly. He then carried this further into another new style called rock 'n' roll.

179

The guitar-picking Pied Piper brought millions of city and rural teen-agers with him, and he began to have an effect on the thinking of arrangers, musicians and recording officials in the country field. Drums were admitted to Grand Ole Opry, and the battle between tradition and modernity grew in intensity.

Presley was far from being the first to reflect a Negro influence in country music. It had been there, in an older and mellower vein, from the very beginning. Jimmie Rodgers, the Carter Family, Hank Williams and many others —including Bill Monroe, the father of the bluegrass style—all have acknowledged a debt to black country musicians, which may account, in part, for the fact that white country music has always had a large colored following in the Southern states. It was no idle coincidence, certainly, that many of Jimmie Rodgers' songs were called blues, and that some of them were in the strict twelve-measure AAB blues form, curiously combined with yodel interludes. On the recording of one of them, "Blue Yodel No. 9," he is backed by Louis Armstrong and Fatha Hines!

But Presley's singing reflected the new urban blues. And, again, it is not a vain coincidence that he broke into recording not from Nashville but from Memphis, which, after the musical decline of Kansas City, had become to the blues what Nashville had long been to country-and-western. His impact on Nashville disclosed, in turn, a conflict between the traditionalists and those who wanted to bring country music up to date comparable to the conflict between the boppers and the "moldy figs" in jazz twenty years earlier.

Not that country music had remained stationary since 1923. It was no longer restricted, even when Presley came along, to the old-time fiddlers, the barn dances and the old ballads. In the process of becoming "country-and-western," it had been infiltrated by a kind of Western, or cowboy, music closer to jazz than any Eastern country music had been. To the nonspecialist, this music is associated with motion-picture horse-opera heroes—Gene Autry, Ken Maynard and Roy Rogers, not to forget Tex Ritter, who sang "High Noon" in the picture of that name. To the historian, however, the less famous name of Bob Wills means more. As leader of a group called the Fort Worth Doughboys, Wills popularized a kind of country dance music that admitted pianos, clarinets, saxophones, various brass instruments, steel guitars and drums, as well as the traditional fiddles. This music came to be known as "western swing."

Billy Charles Malone, a researcher in the field, describing the characteristics of western swing, as quoted by Shelton, says:

Although they used brass occasionally, they did not make their most lasting contribution in this respect. The featured instrument in the Wills organization was the fiddle, the instrument Wills played. Western swing stressed a heavy, insistent beat, the jazz-like improvisation of the steel guitar and the heavily bowed fiddle. It was rhythmically infectious music designed for dancing, but it also stressed lyrics.

An extension of this style survives today in the music of Buck Owens.

A more fatefully influential variant of country music has been the style known as bluegrass, which, in Shelton's words, "built the principal bridge between rural and urban music fans." And as Shelton describes a bluegrass band in action, the reader is likely to superimpose the image and the vocal utterance of Presley and come up with something suggesting rustic Beatles or Rolling Stones:

181

There are five or six colorfully jacketed musicians with string bow ties and broad-brimmed Stetsons. One member of the band, the bassist, probably, is in a tramp's costume, with baggy trousers, galluses and a clown's hat. The bluegrass band clusters in a semi-circle, then almost breaks into a dance as the players bob and weave to get closer to the mike. The faces are placid, unemotional. But the music is not. The banjo crackles with showers of notes flying about like metal confetti in a windstorm. The fiddler whips his bow across the strings, doing daring slides and audacious double stops. The bass is slapped lustily. The Dobro, a steel guitar fretted with a metal bar in the Hawaiian fashion, makes a purring sound. The mandolin, suggesting a brittle, nervous cat walking a telephone wire, scampers at a dangerous speed. Above it all, riding high and penetrating, is a tenor voice, or several voices in two- and three-part harmony. . . .

The most celebrated names in bluegrass have been Bill Monroe, whose native state, Kentucky, and band, the Bluegrass Boys, gave the term to the style, and Earl Scruggs and Lester Flatt, both alumni of the Bluegrass Boys, whose own Foggy Mountain Boys have become even more widely known than the parent organization and whose music gave an authentic period and regional sound to the motion picture, *Bonnie and Clyde*. One of Monroe's songs, "Blue Moon of Kentucky," was, significantly, among the earliest songs recorded by Presley.

Bluegrass is, almost by definition, a traditionalist music, not quite authentic by the earliest criteria of *Grand Ole Opry*, but reactionary in its opposition to contemporary popular influences and especially in its rejection of electrically amplified instruments. It bears some obvious resemblance, in spirit if hardly in style, to the Dixieland revival in jazz; and, because of its resistance to change, it will probably expire as the Dixieland revival did. But its influence is evident today in music far removed from bluegrass, and it will continue to be felt for a long time to come.

Thanks to its having had a greater appeal to urban whites than other styles emanating from *Grand Ole Opry,* bluegrass may be credited with at least an assist in the encouragement of guitar playing and the revival of interest in folk music that have been so prominent a factor in the recent history of American music, particularly among white intellectuals. Another factor, of course, has been the increasing complexity of jazz and the instrumental virtuosity essential to any sort of adequate jazz performance. In this, as in many other respects previously remarked, jazz has emulated the self-destructive procedures of contemporary Serious music.

Modern jazz, insofar as it is written out at all, may not be so difficult to read as a score by Berio or Stockhausen. But what is written out will normally be the smallest part of the assignment. In order to be made effective, its performance will require an improvisatory sophistication far beyond even the exceptionally gifted amateur. In the early days of jazz, in the 1920s and 1930s, every school and college youngster with talent enough to achieve rudimentary facility on piano, drums, trumpet, clarinet or saxophone, could learn to play the new tunes tolerably in a jazz style. In Europe and the British Isles, particularly, this kind of amateur participation survived well into the 1950s and 1960s in what came to be known as traditional jazz.

But this was not satisfactory to the young Americans of the post-World War II generation, to whom traditional jazz already seemed old-fashioned and out-of-date. Nor was this new generation satisfied with what was provided by the professional songwriters and sung by professional singers, good as many of the singers were. The youngsters wanted a music closer to the facts of life; and they found it, initially, in folk music, an area already explored not only in Nashville and in the field of the country blues, but also by such minstrel-researchers as John Jacob Niles, Richard Dyer Bennett, Burl Ives and Alan Lomax. This music was not only more mature in its textual substance; it was also easier to play and easier to sing. It was also easy to compose. A guitar, a few rudimentary chords, a simple tune and a bit of literary invention addressed to a topical theme, and our young man or woman was making his own music.

It may well have been the healthiest thing that had happened in music in several hundred years. Young musical America—its requirements and its tastes ignored by the professionals of both the Serious and the jazz communities—simply took music into its own hands. And it produced, in due course, its own professionals—Bob Dylan, Joan Baez, Simon and Garfunkel and many others. As David P. McAllester, Professor of Anthropology at Wesleyan University, put it in an address to the Tanglewood Symposium of the Music Educators' National Conference in the summer of 1967:

These composer-performer-heroes have a tendency to be self-taught in music. If they learn their techniques from anybody, it is from each other, not the establishment. It is the same with their millions of followers. Yet it should be a stirring thing for anyone concerned with the arts to observe the social and esthetic force of this music. It has become international in scope, and its content is now receiving serious attention from politicians, theologians and philosophers, if not from musicologists. It is not just popular music; it is the music of a social and political movement. . . . Not all of us, or even very many of us older people, can abandon Beethoven and turn on with the Lovin' Spoonful or the Jefferson Airplane. But it is clear that we must give "serious" music a thorough redefinition. The popular music of the teenage subculture *is* serious, and makes a deeply felt statement about life.

What had originated in more or less pure folk music could not remain immune to contemporary fashion, any more than the urban black community could go on forever singing field hollers and twelve-measure blues. Drums and a double bass—symbols of the inevitability, the depth and the pervasiveness of the African element in the new American music—were added to the guitar to produce what became known variously as folk rock, Elizabethan rock, Baroque rock, and so on. The music was tending toward something not too far removed from the combination of rhythm-and-blues and country-and-western represented by Presley. More refined, possibly, even a little bland, but not essentially either dissimilar or incompatible.

The ultimate congregation of these diverse strains—country and urban blues, gospel song, rock 'n' roll, country-and-western, bluegrass, folk and even the close-harmony vocal techniques of such earlier popular groups as the Four Freshmen, the Hi Los, the Weavers—was accomplished in the 1960s by the most improbable and unpredictable of all conceivable agents: a ragtag quartet from Liverpool, England, called the Beatles.

Again, it was not that the Beatles were so startlingly original. They were not, in fact, initially, at least, original at all. But they were musical, adaptable and imaginative in their selection and processing of sources and models. They were very catholic, too, drawing, not indiscriminately but without inhibition, on everything that appealed to them from gospel song and country music to the string quartet and the electronic devices of contemporary Serious composition.

The Beatles were not by any means the first to blend the

distinctive and sometimes divisive characteristics of black and white in the various categories of American music. There had always been, as noted previously, an African strain in American country music; and the various forms of the blues were not all purely black. They had all drawn upon Euro-American scales, harmonies, rhythms, instruments and song forms. Many Negro artists had addressed themselves successfully to a large white public—Duke Ellington, Louis Armstrong, Count Basie, Ethel Waters, Ella Fitzgerald, Lena Horne, Nat King Cole, Harry Belafonte and, most recently, Ray Charles. All of them had adapted an essentially African musicality to the musical experience and requirements of their European-oriented white listeners. In the music of certain white artists, conversely, there was more of the African influence than in that of many black musicians. Long before Elvis Presley, there had been Mildred Bailey and Connee Boswell, and after Presley had come Jerry Lee Lewis, Carl Perkins, Buddy Holly and Johnny Rivers.

The trend among the younger white musicians—when the Beatles came along, and discounting the "folkies"—was to work close to the new urban blues style, much as Benny Goodman, Bix Beiderbecke, Jack Teagarden, Bunny Berigan, Eddie Condon and many others had worked close to the New Orleans–Chicago jazz style of the late 1920s and early 1930s. And, again, some dilution was required if this music were to be made palatable to a more or less universal white audience. Just as early jazz, in its purer forms, had been a bit too exotic for the white majority, so, in the late 1950s, the rocking beat, the ecstatic singing and shouting and honking, the swiveling gyration of hips and knees and the often bawdy lyrics of an urban blues-based rock 'n' roll were too randy for general dissemination, however appealing to a large segment of the younger white generation.

Dilution had been accomplished in the 1920s by the Paul Whitemans, the Fred Warings and the Guy Lombardos, and in the 1930s by swing and the jazz-flavored styling of popular songs. Now, in the 1960s, and for the first time, synthesis came from abroad. England had been following the American lead for the better part of the century. First Jack Hylton, then Ted Heath and Ray Noble, and, finally, John Dankworth, had developed first-rate big bands, while the older style had been—and still is—perpetuated by Humphrey Lyttleton, now reinforced by Chris Barber and Alex Welsh. Tommy Steele had followed almost immediately on the heels —or hips—of Presley. The folk song movement has had an outstanding representative in Donovan (Leitch), and even the urban blues a determined and accomplished champion in John Mayall. But with the Beatles, the non-American was more than an imitator.

Never previously had an alien performer or group exerted a decisive influence on American music. The Beatles' style may have been only a synthesis of American strains, with an occasional suggestion of the music hall for good measure; but as a synthesis it was both novel and widely attractive—so attractive, indeed, that "pop," a British term as used in this context, was accepted into the otherwise exclusively American terminology of American music.

The ingredients have been variously identified, which is not to be wondered at when one notes the great variety of style embraced in the Beatles' long succession of LPs and singles. They were originally pretty well founded on rock, with the usual suggestions of gospel song and country-and-western. But some of their earlier records revive more distant memories—spirituals, the Hall Johnson Choir and a kind of ballad which, without the modern rhythmic trimmings, could have been sung by John McCormack.

More recently they have tapped Indian music, the string quartet, and even the symphony orchestra. Frederic V. Grunfeld, an American critic, in an article in *Horizon* (summer, 1967), has called them "the great syncretists and mixmasters of our day." Their finest record, "Sgt Pepper's Lonely Hearts Club Band," supports this description. Their work since then, says Grunfeld, "is a great eclectic circus of Indian raga, Salivation Army, Benjamin British, tailgate, gutbucket and aleatoric chance-music, all handled without hang-ups or uptightness."

Initially, it would seem, the tumultuous popularity of the Beatles could be attributed to the wistful lyricism they brought to a kind of music that tended, in both its white rural and its black urban American sources, to be rambunctious, unruly and uninhibited, or at least to be felt as such by the white urban middle class. The Beatles retained the vitality of the rock style while polishing the surface and rounding the edges. And there was something irresistibly appealing about these four boys from the poorer sections of such an unlikely place as Liverpool.

Perhaps it was inevitable [wrote John Gabree in *Down Beat* (November 16, 1967)] that the revitalization of pop music would occur through a medium, the Beatles, that filtered out the elements that mass cultists found offensive. . . . They were fresh, while American pop music hadn't produced a new face of lasting significance in a half-dozen years. They had a good ear for harmony, and a near-perfect sense of taste when choosing whom to imitate. They sounded raw and vital when compared with their vapid contemporaries in the Top 40 stations. But they were also safe, being white and having none of the aggressive sexuality that had been so upsetting in the likes of Elvis—all they wanted to do, remember, was hold your hand.

This is certainly one of the reasons why the Beatles, from the very first, reached, and were found acceptable by, a larger audience than had existed for any of the various styles from which they worked. As they matured, and as their production grew in variety and sophistication, their appeal spread to an intellectual audience that had never before had ears for any Popular style or personality.

Serious-music critics—but only, of course, the very few who listen—have detected qualities in the music of the Beatles and some of their imitators, both British and American, that escaped them in even the most sophisticated achievements of jazz. William Mann, music critic of the London *Times,* for instance, whose interest had already been aroused by Presley and Bill Haley's Comets, and who has followed the Beatles with enlightened critical attention from the beginning, was led by "Sgt Pepper's Lonely Hearts Club Band" to foresee a new kind of integrated LP, "a popsong cycle, a Tin Pan Alley *Dichterliebe.*" This was a portentous observation, for it pointed the way to the achievement of larger forms and a counter to the familiar argument of the Serious-music community that Popular music could not be taken seriously until it could stretch out beyond the single song format.

Wilfrid Mellers wrote in the *Guardian* that this was precisely what the Beatles had done in "Sgt Pepper." It was, he said, a song cycle about loneliness. And Edward Greenfield, also in the *Guardian,* offered the opinion that the Beatles "have written more memorable tunes since the war than anyone except Benjamin Britten," an observation that some might find flattering to Britten. Grunfeld, in his *Horizon* article, carried hyperbole a bit farther by describing the final chord of "A Day in the Life"—the last band of "Sgt Pepper"— as the most definitive final chord in the history of music. It alone, he wrote, "is worth the price of admission; nobody else, not even Rachmaninoff, carried off a *Schlussakkord* with such panache."

The chord is played by a symphony orchestra, and Grunfeld may have had this fact in mind, as well as the string quartet that plays so eloquent a part in the instrumental backing for "She's Leaving Home" on the same record, when he went on to say:

The Beatles have already succeeded in bringing the two mainstreams of music flowing back in the same broad channel—something that has not happened for about three hundred years. . . . When the revolution is complete and the millennium arrives, the art of music will once more be a continuum instead of a series of soundproof compartments. For a generation bent on enlarging the continuum of its sensations, the Beatles have permanently expanded the limits of the world we live in, the world of vibrations.

They have expanded it, certainly, although their most important contribution may prove to have been the expansion of the audience for the new trends in Popular music. It is unlikely, I think, that they have unified music. The very multiplicity and diversity of their sources suggest rather a transitional contiguity. Their sources have been tapped, not drained, and the sources continue in their own path, influenced, perhaps, by the Beatles and by the Beatles' imitators, but still retaining a separate identity.

The Beatles may, nevertheless, prove to have been the source, in turn, of a new mainstream. Too much has been made, I think, of their eclecticism and not enough of the extent to which they have been drawn upon by other and now younger eclectics. Since the Beatles' emergence in the early 1960s, thousands of groups have been founded in their image, all called the This, the That and the Other Thing, and all of them sounding more or less like the Beatles. It is all very well to contend, as Gabree does, that some of the later groups are, in one respect or another, the Beatles' superiors. This may be true. But it remains a fact that the Beatles have been both a summation and a beginning.

In them were assembled, for the first time, all the various and diverse elements of American music in the midcentury except jazz, and from these elements are now emerging a number of derivatives, some looking back to ballad, to folk song, to Baroque and to Medieval, others forward to new exploration in the areas of instrumental experimentation and electronics. Both in the use of advanced recording techniques and in the recall of Renaissance and Medieval melodic and harmonic procedures, the pop groups are working parallel with some Serious composers—Carl Orff, Krzysztof Penderecki, Peter Maxwell Davies—who have, apparently, sensed the utter sterility of serialism and are seeking a way back to a more musical music.

Left high and dry in this evolutionary maelstrom was jazz. Accustomed by years of flattering critical attention—although not from the musical Establishment, of course—and honored by the State Department and the United States Information Agency, however hypocritically and opportunistically, as ambassadors of the American Way of Life, jazz musicians felt themselves as Artists, immune from the currents of Popular music; and they remained, for fifteen years, hostile or indifferent to what was taking place all around them. As Ralph Gleason put it, in the September 1967 issue of *Jazz & Pop:* "It is a curious thing that jazz began by accusing the symphony and conservatory players of refusing to listen to them. Now the jazz musicians, or at least a regrettable majority of them, are not opening their ears to the worthwhile music coming from the new generation."

191

They had their eyes opened, if not their ears, when, in the summer of 1967, the two leading American jazz periodicals opened their pages to rock and pop. First was *Down Beat.* In a "Message to Our Readers" in the issue of June 29, Dan Morgenstern, the editor, came out with it:

For well over a decade, the music world has been living—for better or worse—with a phenomenon called rock 'n' roll. At first, it was often for the worse, but now it is increasingly for the better. The music has become a medium for creative expression undreamed of when Bill Haley began to rock around the clock. Undeniably, rock 'n' roll has come of age, as the nomenclature indicates: folk-rock, blues-rock, raga-rock, psychedelic-rock and even jazz-rock. . . . *Down Beat,* without reducing its coverage of jazz, will expand its editorial perspective to include the musically valid aspects of the rock scene.

A month later, in its August issue, *Jazz* became *Jazz & Pop,* the transformation covered by an editorial:

Jazz, pop, classical, folk . . . these are crude descriptive categories at best, and they better apply to the in-group exclusiveness of their audiences than to musical sounds. At least so far as the music is concerned, there are no neat boundaries. Only classical music seems to hold itself aloof, supported by moneyed individuals, academic institutions, foundations and governments—it is (like it or not) *the* music of the Establishment. And this has more to do with class sources of the music than with the music itself. The other three—jazz, pop and folk—are children of the streets: without official recognition, scuffling for survival at times, they still go on speaking to the largest audience in the world.

Let's face it. Jazz needs popular music. Economically as well as esthetically, they have *always* interpenetrated each other, the pop song becoming the jazz vehicle, the jazz artist becoming popular musician. Let's forget categories as much as we can, and remember that music, first of all, is that great transcendentalist that has been blowing minds, salving souls and telling us where we've been at for all of human history. To paraphrase Bob Dylan, "It's all music, man!"

The editorial may have been stimulated by Philip Elwood's coverage, in the same issue, of the first Monterey Pop Festival. The principal people noticeably absent, he noted, were the jazz fans and writers, and he went on to say:

This is a good indication of what is wrong in jazz: those who write about it too often also define it. And their definitions usually are as limited as their own interests. I heard more improvisation and individual creativity at the Pop Festival (alas!) than I have heard at many recent jazz events. . . . Some of the jazz stuffed shirts had better awaken to the realization that it is their narrow definitions, and not the music itself, that have stifled jazz in recent years. . . . Today's younger generation are not just going to create their own music—they are going to teach an older generation a few things about how to appreciate it, besides.

An example of such instruction was a drastic reversal of the British Broadcasting Corporation's radio programming policy at about the same time that *Down Beat* and *Jazz* were changing editorial policy. The BBC's patrician indifference to pop had led to the establishment of a fleet of pirate stations in the North Sea, broadcasting commercially sponsored pop programs to eager British—and Continental—listeners in defiance of the BBC monopoly. Parliament passed legislation forbidding British firms to participate in this freebooting exercise; but in the end the BBC had to capitulate and make of BBC-1 a pop station, staffing it with disc jockeys recruited from the pirate stations.

The basic lesson for the older generation of jazz fans—and it will be just as hard to swallow as the error of serialism is hard for the Serious composer and Serious-music critic to swallow—is that pop music did not deviate from the mainstream of Western musical evolution. Jazz did. There are, to be sure, various ways of plotting the mainstream in our century, depending upon where one's interest and enthusiasm lie. The jazz musician thinks in terms of ragtime to New Orleans and Dixieland through swing to bop and the New Jazz. Those closer to what the jazz musician regards as the popular scene think in terms of sweet to swing to the singers to Tijuana Brass and Al Hirt. But listening to the newest sounds, including the British, one can trace, I suspect, an even more decisive current running from New Orleans and country blues through the union of jazz and blues in Kansas City to rhythm-and-blues and the urban blues of Memphis and Chicago to rock.

The vital, continually rejuvenating force in the American mainstream has been the musicality of the Afro-American, both melodic and rhythmic. Popular music, in the last decade particularly, has become more African. Keil, in his *Urban Blues,* has been more perceptive about this, and more explicit, than any other writer whose work has come to my attention:

It is simply incontestable that year by year, American popular music has come to sound more and more like African popular music. The rhythmic complexity and subtlety, the emphasis on percussive sound qualities, the call-and-response pattern, the characteristic vocal elements (shout, growl, falsetto and so on), blues chromaticism, blues and gospel chord progressions, Negro vocabulary, Afro-American dance steps—all have become increasingly prominent in American music. If empirical evidence is

194

wanted, simply turn on the radio or television, or sample the best-selling records of the day, and you will be immersed in the results of the appropriation-revitalization process. . . .

It is also worth noting that the white copies of Negro originals show greater skill, sensitivity and fidelity than ever before. The young Chicagoans Paul Butterfield and Elvin Bishop are well on their way toward mastering the rough city blues idiom typified by Muddy Waters and Howlin' Wolf, just as the young Chicagoans Bix Beiderbecke, Eddie Condon, George Wettling and friends learned the New Orleans jazz style brought to the Windy City by King Oliver and Louis Armstrong almost fifty years earlier. . . . I find it increasingly difficult to separate white and Negro performers, largely because many Negro stylists have eliminated some of the coarser qualities from the blues and gospel styles they draw upon for material, while a number of white performers have perfected their handling of Negro vocal accent, inflection patterns and phrasing.

Including the white British performers. As a resident of London, and a consistent listener to BBC-1 and BBC-TV, as well as to records, I have been astonished, especially in interview-performance programs, to hear English boys speaking cockney and various other regional inflections but singing in pure American urban Negro without a trace of English accent, just as Petula Clark, for instance, speaks English but sings American songs in white American.

The mainstream of Western music has, in any case, become increasingly hospitable to its African tributary, so much so, in fact, that now, as we reach the end of the 1960s, there might be some question as to which is tributary and which is mainstream. And the vitality of the African contribution, at the same time, has been continually stimulated by Negro resentment of the appropriation by white American and

British musicians of the Negro's distinctive characteristics. This resentment had more than a little to do with bop, although exclusion here was extended to inferior black musicians as well as to white. It had everything to do with the evolution of soul music.

Negro music, since the days of the first recordings [says Keil], but especially during the last two decades, has become progressively more "reactionary"—that is, more African in its essentials—primarily because the various blues and jazz styles are, at least in their initial phases, symbolic referents of in-group solidarity for the black masses and the more intellectual segments of the black bourgeoisie. It is for this reason that each successive appropriation and commercialization of a Negro style by white America through its record industry and mass media has stimulated the Negro community and its spokesmen to generate a "new" music that it can call its own. In every instance the new music has been an amalgamation of increased musical knowledge (technically speaking) and a re-emphasis of the most basic Afro-American resources.

Any assessment of the implications of this appropriation-revitalization process, as illustrated in jazz and rock, and in the occasional juxtaposition of these styles and any kind of Serious music, must proceed from an acknowledgment that, in Keil's words, "in the blending process the African rhythmic foundation absorbs and transforms the European elements." This applies not only to Serious music but even to jazz, in which the European elements are more pronounced than in the blues or in the various forms of rock, which are all derived from the blues.

Jazz will have to come to terms with rock, and some of the younger jazz musicians, both white and black—Gary Burton, Larry Coryell, Gabor Szabo, John Handy, Jeremy Steig and

Charles Lloyd, for example—are already showing the way. There are no insuperable problems; for the styles are idiomatically, if not yet intellectually, compatible. The rock musician can use the jazz musician's superior instrumental sophistication, while the jazz musician can find salvation from both excessive intellectuality and anarchy in the rhythmic, melodic and textual vitality of rock.

The prospect would seem to be for an increasing sophistication of rock and pop, embracing the jazz musician and, possibly, the electronically oriented Serious composer, too, With the movement of Serious composition from the sclerotic dogma of serialism into the uncharted frontiers of electronics, the sense of a continuing European tradition is no longer so pervasive as to render the European and the Afro-American idioms congenitally incompatible. Young rock musicians, too, have been drawn to electronics, especially to the collage techniques of *musique concrète*. The Serious composer has tended to be scientific and to concentrate on experimentation for experiment's sake. The pop and rock musicians have used electronics and collage more musically. But there is no reason, now, why the Serious composer might not apply the fruits of his laboratories to decently musical purpose.

As Joe Butler, of the Lovin' Spoonful, has expressed it, "There is going to be more and more trading of ideas in all areas of music. Different people will be meeting each other. Music is getting more like music, and it's getting harder and harder to categorize a piece of music." It's also getting harder and harder for the layman—or even for the insider—to sort it all out. The music of the Lovin' Spoonful, for example, has been described as a mixture of Delta blues, Sousa marches, Bob Dylan, jazz, rhythm-and-blues and country-and-western. Alfred G. Aronowitz, in an article on pop in the July 15,

1967, *Saturday Evening Post,* was not exaggerating when he wrote:

By the middle of 1967, American's pop music scene had become as incomprehensible to the people who dreamed it all up as it is to the people who are sleeping through it. . . . It is as if some magician had started pulling tricks out of a hat and found, to his amazement, that the hat contained more surprises than his magic could account for.

It is possible to infer from observations such as these that pop, or rock, may be entering a period in which white influences will again lead the new music away from its elementally musical African roots. According to Keil, it would be for the last time in the century-long process of appropriation-revitalization, which he sees now in its final phase. He may well be right about this. But it is also possible that white influences may now be more vigorously rooted.

The white musician, attracted by the vitality and the creative imagination of the American Negro's music, has, in the past, had little of his own to offer. But now, emancipated at last from the esthetic conventions and from the no longer fruitful musical procedures of the older European idiom, he is discovering a hitherto frustrated creativity. The new younger generation, both black and white, is making its own music on its own terms—not just on the musician's terms, but on terms valid for the entire generation.

Given this new circumstance, and the wealth of talent already visible in the white contribution, it seems not impossible that the future may see less dilution and something more like an even exchange, embracing the young Serious composer and musician, too, as reflected in the mature records of the Beatles.

The Lyric Theater

THE PRESENT and future of opera, for fully half a century, have been the despair of everyone concerned with Serious music. And not without reason. The last operas to achieve enduring public acceptance were *Wozzeck* and *Turandot,* dating respectively from 1925 and 1926. With them, the evolutionary cycle of Europe's contribution to the history of the lyric theater was complete.

Nor can the acceptance of *Wozzeck* and *Turandot* be acknowledged without qualification. As stalwarts of the repertoire they can hardly be equated with *Salome, Elektra, Der Rosenkavalier,* or with *La Bohème, Madama Butterfly* and *Tosca.* Like Strauss's later operas, both *Wozzeck* and *Turandot* seem not so much a resurgence as a last gasp.

Many operas have been written and produced in the intervening years, probably several hundred. Some, such as Stravinsky's *The Rake's Progress,* Menotti's *The Consul* and Benjamin Britten's *Peter Grimes,* have enjoyed a tenuous vogue. The sponsorship of new operas has been accepted as a moral obligation by the administrators of public and private funds. Critics have been hopefully indulgent, and the public has approached each new offering with a greater readiness to applaud, or to withhold censure, than was accorded opera composers when Rossini, Donizetti, Meyerbeer, Wagner and Verdi were young men.

But for all this benevolent encouragement, opera composers have been no more able than symphony composers to appeal to the hearts and the minds of the general Serious-music public. The composer's problem is the same whether he writes an opera or a symphony. If he attempts the kind of melodious and harmonious music that audiences treasure in the older masterpieces, he appears old-fashioned and imitative. If he writes the kind of music that will gain him recognition as a modernist among the arbiters of musical fashion, he may achieve status but he loses the public.

It is one of the many paradoxes of contemporary musical life—and it applies to jazz as well as to Serious music—that a composer, or, as in jazz, the performer-creator or composer-arranger, can enjoy a certain popularity without being fashionable—a Menotti, for example, or a George Shearing—while others, of more purposefully adventurous or dogmatically experimental disposition—Boulez, Stockhausen and Cage, or Ornette Coleman and Archie Shepp—can become fashionable without being popular.

Unless, of course, he works in an unfashionable field. A considerable number of gifted and accomplished composers are doing precisely that, uninhibited by expert scrutiny and stylistic insecurity; and it is in their work that one may find, I believe, the lyric theater of our own time. It is right where it ought to be: in the contemporary theater, *i.e.,* on the motion-picture screen of the public theater and the private living room.

General and critical appreciation of this music is discouraged by a formidable complex of folklore and prejudice, derived primarily from the superstition that there is something indecent in the association of art and commerce. The musician—to speak only of music—who tailors his product to commercial objectives and commercial requirements is promptly, almost automatically and axiomatically, put down as a prostitute.

The composer who writes for motion pictures, television serials and radio and television commercials would appear to be an especially low form of prostitute. Not only does he wittingly serve a commercial purpose; he also works in a medium in which music is given a subordinate role. How is it possible, the Serious-music critic will ask, for music to be good when the composer must accede to the wishes of a producer, when he is governed in matters of substance and style by what seems appropriate to story, setting or product, when he must trim his contribution to what is permitted by a budget, and accept editing and abbreviation as directed by higher authority?

Well, it is possible, of course. It always has been possible, and most of the great European composers did it, especially the composers who have worked in the theater—Handel, Gluck, Mozart, Rossini, Weber, Donizetti, Bellini, Meyerbeer, Verdi and Wagner. Some of these men, late in their careers, and from positions of power and authority based on earlier accomplishment, could dictate conditions and terms. But initially, at least, they had to make concessions to budgets, singers, censors, mistresses and prevailing trends in privileged and popular taste.

The composer, today, who writes for films—or for television serials and commercials—has an additional handicap in a fifty-year-old tradition of inferior music. The studios where their music is produced have been slow to discover that good and original music pays; and the conspicuous odor of hackwork that society as a whole assumes to be inherent in the craft of film scoring has certainly been notable in most of its previous history. Since one of the purposes of music written to accompany pictures is that it not call attention to itself, it should not be surprising that many splendid achievements of the past decade have gone unremarked by motion-picture critics, Serious-music critics or jazz critics.

But the motion picture, more than any other form of theater except ballet, requires music, and it was inevitable that it would eventually find its own contemporary music, shaped by the musical taste and experience of an enormous contemporary film-going public. Motion-picture producers and exhibitors were aware of the musical requirement from the very beginning, first to fill the silences of the silent picture, and subsequently to heighten pictorial sensation and dramatic tension, which has been the role of music in the theater since the dawn of theater history. One speaks today in the advertising world of music's capacity to provide "emotional memorability." No one thought in those terms in the early days of the motion picture, but the capacity was there, as it has always been, and it has been solicited and exploited accordingly.

Many of us can still remember the Saturday night picture in the local hall or parish house, with the pianist seated in a corner by the screen, playing whatever came into his head or seemed appropriate to what was taking place in the film ("Home, Sweet Home" for a slapstick representation of a domestic quarrel) . A next step was the issuance of cue sheets to give the pianist or organist a better-thought-out, less haphazard guide than the spur-of-the-moment impulses of his own judgment, ingenious as these often were. In the larger urban houses there might be a reasonably well-organized score played by organs or orchestras. Then came synchronization with a recorded score (*e.g.*, Erno Rapee's music for *Sunrise* and Henry Hadley's for *Don Juan*), followed shortly by the talking picture. With Al Jolson's *The Jazz Singer* (1927) the way was opened for the highly organized lyric theater that we have in the motion picture today.

This organization was not achieved overnight, nor is it now by any means complete. Listening to the new pictures, however, and comparing the scores with those of older pictures shown on television, one is struck immediately by the old-fashioned sound of the old pictures. One forgets, or has never been made to realize, that the old-fashioned sound was once new—at least in the pictures—and that what we hear today in the new pictures is the product of a long and tentative evolution retarded by the fact that music's destiny in the motion pictures, while determined by the public in the long run, has been guided from day to day and from picture to picture by individuals who knew little about music and cared less.

I was reminded of this not long ago when I ran across an article written by George Antheil for *Modern Music* in 1936. Antheil was one of a number of Serious composers who sensed the musical potentiality of motion pictures, and he devoted most of his mature career to score writing. In 1936 he had just produced a notable score for *The Plainsman,* and his experiences prompted him to predict that his example in going to Hollywood would be followed by other Serious composers, not, he emphasized, because the producers *want* better music but "because they need it."

> First of all [he wrote], it is cheaper to write an authentic and exciting musical background than it is to build an equally authentic and exciting background set. Werner Janssen's Chinese music lifted at least $50,000 off the budget of *The General*

Died at Dawn. When good scores begin to do things like this, they talk to Hollywood in its own language—the language of money. Secondly, the great movie publics of the world are gradually becoming accustomed to better-fitting scores, scores that are especially calculated for the needs of each picture and not dragged out of the pages of Schubert's Unfinished Symphony. Today a good score is as essential to a production as good photography. Attempt, for instance, to foist a 1929-style score or a 1929-style photography upon the present-day movie public, and you will be surprised how immediately they protest. The truth of movie-music is becoming apparent; slowly, and with infinite patience, music is going forward with our new shadowy pictures and their miraculous sound effects.

Constant Lambert, in *Music Ho!* two years earlier, had written:

The cinema is undoubtedly the most important of the mechanical stimuli offered to the composer of today; and in spite of its ephemeral nature, it is the only art whose progress is not, at the moment, dispiriting to watch. While the music of today seems either to be a romantic swan song regretting past days, as in Delius; an alembicated and intellectual crossword puzzle, as in von Webern, or a callow reflection of the drab minutiae of daily life, as in Hindemith, the films, with superb insolence, have blended old-fashioned naïveté of sentiment with up-to-the-minute sophistication of technique, producing, as if by accident, the most vigorous art form of today.

Films have the emotional impact for the twentieth century that operas had for the nineteenth. Pudovkin and Eisenstein are the true successors of Moussorgsky; D. W. Griffiths is our Puccini, Cecil B. De Mille our Meyerbeer, and René Clair our Offenbach. It is not exaggerating to say that a film like King Vidor's *Hallelujah* has a far greater esthetic significance than any opera written since the war, and that the pickax spiritual in *I Am a*

204

Fugitive is, in its medium, worthy to be compared with the chorus crying for bread in the original version of *Boris Godounov.*

Lambert was speaking of producers and directors rather than musicians, and he adds that, while Pudovkin and Eisenstein were the spiritual successors of Moussorgsky, there was, unfortunately, no Moussorgsky to write music for them. By the time composers had discovered the new medium, he noted, they were too late. Their first great opportunity had been in that brief interval when the synchronized score did not have to contend with the spoken word. When pictures began to talk, music "was banished except as an invisible and improbable accompaniment to love scenes, and purely realistic synchronized sound took its place."

The prospect was not so bleak as Lambert had imagined, but there can be no doubt that composing for films became less attractive to the Serious composer—aside from the financial reward—than it might have been had pictures remained forever mute. Progress was slow, even slower, probably, than Antheil had anticipated. There was no sudden emigration of Serious composers to Hollywood and the film capitals of Europe. Some tried their hands at it, and by no means without success—Antheil, Aaron Copland, Virgil Thomson, Ernst Toch, Erich Korngold, Miklós Rósza and Leonard Bernstein in the United States; Artur Honegger, Darius Milhaud, Henri Sauguet, Georges Auric and Jacques Ibert in France; Sergei Prokofiev and Dmitri Shostakovich in the Soviet Union, and Paul Dessau, Hanns Eisler and Karol Rathaus in central Europe. All were following, probably unwittingly, in the footsteps of Camille Saint-Saëns, who had composed incidental music for a French film, *L'Assassinat du Duc de Guise* (Opus 128), as early as 1908.

But almost without exception they grew impatient of the

frustrations and disciplines and unenlightened outside inter-
ference associated with film scoring. As Copland, the most
successful and persistent of them, put it in *Our New Music:*

Essentially, there is nothing about the movie medium to rule
out any composer with a dramatic imagination. But the man who
insists on complete self-expression had better stay home and
write symphonies. He will never be happy in Hollywood.

But he added, cogently:

The best one can say about Hollywood is that it is a place
where composers are actually needed. The accent is entirely on
the living composer. With the radio and the phonograph, the
music track of the sound film must be set down as a revolution-
izing force in today's music.

The men who dominated the formative years of film scoring were a different breed—excellent musicians, most of
them, well versed in the traditional techniques of composition and instrumentation, and certainly familiar with the
traditional literature, but without pretensions of significant
originality. Indeed, their very want of originality enhanced
their value. The purpose of music in the pictures, during
those intermediate years and excepting, of course, motion-
picture musicals, was to be effective without being obtrusive;
and in order to be effective it had also to be familiar. Thus it
was that most sound-track music was reminiscent of Wagner,
Tchaikovsky, Strauss, Debussy, Ravel, the early Stravinsky
and Prokofiev. And thus it was, inevitably, that most contemporary concert and opera music of the period that was
neither severely neoclassical nor dogmatically dodecaphonic
suggested the sound track.

It may, indeed, be premature to speak of this type of composer and of this type of composition in the past tense. A

second generation of symphonically oriented composers still works—and works well—from a stylistic base in the older conventions of film scoring: Elmer Bernstein, Ernest Gold, Jerry Goldsmith, Bernard Herrmann, Kenyon Hopkins, Maurice Jarre, Bronislav Kaper, Sol Kaplan, André Previn, David Raksin, Leonard Rosenman and Nino Rota. But alongside them, and competing with them, is a still-younger generation, of strikingly different background and orientation.

Among the composers I have in mind, and some of the pictures with which they have established their reputations and indicated a new philosophy of film scoring, are: John Barry (*The Ipcress File, The Knack, Séance on a Wet Afternoon* and *The Whisperers*); Luis Bonfa (*Black Orpheus*); John Dankworth (*Saturday Night and Sunday Morning* and *Darling*); Dave Grusin (*Divorce American Style*); Chico Hamilton (*Sweet Smell of Success* and *Repulsion*); Herbie Hancock (*Blow-up*); Neal Hefti (*Barefoot in the Park*); Quincy Jones (*The Pawnbroker, In the Heat of the Night* and *In Cold Blood*); Michel LeGrand (*The Umbrellas of Cherbourg*); Henry Mancini (*Breakfast at Tiffany's, The Pink Panther* and *Hatari*); Johnny Mandel (*I Want to Live* and *The Sandpiper*); Alex North (*A Streetcar Named Desire*); Sonny Rollins (*Alfie*); Eddie Sauter (*Mickey One*); Lalo Schifrin (*To Catch a Thief*); and Leith Stevens (*The Wild One*).

Significant facts emerge from a list such as this. The composers are, almost without exception, jazz-oriented. This in itself would represent a departure from the older conventions of film scoring, including the scoring of musicals. But what makes it the more remarkable is that none of these films is a musical, nor are the scores specifically or exclusively jazz. The composers, moreover, while most of them have been known primarily as jazz composer-arrangers, are all conservatory-trained, or have supplemented the skills acquired in the pragmatic school of the jazz composer-arranger through private study of traditional European techniques. One of the older school of film scorers remarked to me that the younger men were "bandleaders who have learned to write for strings." This is true in most cases, but the quality of their writing defies the implied disparagement. Many of them could teach their elders a thing or two about writing for winds.

Nor is it without significance that this list is by no means exclusively American. Barry and Dankworth are English; Bonfa is Brazilian; LeGrand is French; and Schifrin, now an American, is Argentine-born and Paris-trained (Charles Koechlin and Olivier Messaien). To the list might be added the Swedes Bengt Hallberg and Bengt-Arne Wallin, the Greek Manos Hadjidakis and the English Johnny Keating.

Common to all their scores, despite the variety of schooling, experience and natural origin, is the pulse of jazz, the jazz arranger's skill in the most effective use of a small number of instruments and the virtuosity of the jazz musician in applying the appropriate insinuation to the given phrase or cadence. Inevitably, the composer-arrangers have brought with them to the studios a number of outstanding jazz musicians, who alone know how to read the arranger's "chart." Mandel, for example, wrote simply "Miles" over a certain trumpet passage in *The Sandpiper,* meaning that he wanted his soloist to play it in the style of Miles Davis. This would have meant nothing to most symphony trumpeters; but for Jack Sheldon, who was playing it, this was all he needed to be told. It has been observed—by Mancini—that if you want to hear again one of Woody Herman's famous Herds, the likeliest place would be a Los Angeles studio.

What one hears in this type of score—or reacts to without

consciously hearing—is rarely jazz in any usual or specific sense of the term. Almost entirely missing is the element of improvisation. The coordination and timing of the motion-picture underscore—a term more common now than "sound track"—is too tight to permit inspirational excursions. The new style of underscore is more likely to be a music distilled from the instrumental techniques and the pulse of jazz, but employing, where suitable, all the devices of Serious music, even including, as in Dankworth's score for *Accident,* serial techniques.

The jazz musicians who play these scores are as literate as the men who write them; and, like the writers, most of them have classical schooling. They can—idiomatically and stylistically—work both sides of the street. The older, symphony-oriented composers and musicians—with some exceptions—cannot. In the music that one hears today in the motion pictures, television serials, and even in radio and television commercials may be discerned the first promising evidence of an ultimate conjunction of the American and what still remains of the old European mainstream in Western music.

Neither the Serious composer, attempting to absorb or exploit the infections vitality of jazz (Milhaud, Křenek, Stravinsky, Copland, Liebermann), nor the jazz composer-arranger, attempting to achieve respectability by drawing upon the symphony orchestra and classical forms (Ellington, Teo Macero, Robert Graettinger, William Russo, Pete Rugolo, John Lewis and Stan Kenton) had previously been able to accomplish anything but an unsatisfactory hybrid. Nor have the so-called Third Stream exercises of the past decade, most notably Gunther Schuller's opera, *The Visitation,* shown much promise.

Some of us had thought, for a time, that conjunction might take place in the Broadway musical. But the musical atrophied before the American idiom came of age. There was compatibility of a kind, but it was closer to coexistence than to conjunction or confluence. While accepting the jazz pulse and exploiting, where appropriate, a jazz instrumentation and the jazz musician's way of phrasing, the American musical never cut itself off entirely from its European roots. Upbeat numbers were less jazz than merely jazzy. And the strings were always there for the sentimental situation. Hundreds of songs from the musicals became jazz standards. But they were subjected by jazz musicians and by jazz and Popular singers to a style of performance very different from that given them originally in the theater.

And the musical was, curiously, more American in its youth than in its maturity. It became pretentious in the midcentury, and less idiomatic musically. There was an increasing emphasis upon story line, production and integration; and in the last musicals of Rodgers and Hammerstein, it was closer to light opera and operetta than it had been in the innocent days when half a dozen memorable songs by Berlin, Kern, Gershwin, Youmans, Schwartz, Arlen, Porter and Rodgers could carry a show and give it a special American flavor.

If the motion-picture underscore has been late in emerging as a more promising area of reconciliation and conjunction, it may well be because neither the motion picture nor the state of jazz composition—as opposed to jazz performance—was previously ready for it. Hollywood, during the era of the big studios, was hardly noted either for musical enlightenment or for a spirit of commercial adventure. Even the film versions of musicals were presented very much as they had been presented on Broadway, with the orchestration much glossier and the production numbers more sumptuous. For the nonmusical motion picture, the conventional symphony orchestra background met the requirements.

The breakthrough came with the more or less coincidental appearance of the independent motion-picture producer and the skilled and literate jazz composer-arranger. It also coincided with the early prosperity of television, which brought with it a new and insatiable demand for effective underscores written in a contemporary and colloquial idiom. Advertisers discovered the value of music as a persuasive and associative element in the presentation of merchandise. And in the television medium especially, the need became apparent for a kind of music closer to the lives and the experience of a mass audience than the warmed-over symphonic and semiclassical fare of the traditional motion-picture sound track or the huckster's trivial jingle.

The economics of film production also played a role. With the cost of a symphony orchestra of upwards of fifty musicians rising from year to year, producers, especially the smaller and more adventurous of them, were well disposed to a new approach to scoring, particularly if it could save—or even make —money. Two influential pictures were *The Third Man,* with nothing more than Antal Karas's zither and such haunting tunes as the "Harry Lime Theme" and "Mozart Café," and *High Noon,* which demonstrated the value of a single song capable not only of supporting the picture but also of becoming a money-maker in its own right. This was also true of *La Ronde.*

More important, from a purely musical point of view, were Franz Waxman's jazz score for *Crime in the Streets,* Elmer Bernstein's score (with Shorty Rogers' Giants) for *The Man with the Golden Arm;* Johnny Mandel's score for *I Want to Live,* exploiting the Gerry Mulligan Quartet, and Alex North's score for *A Streetcar Named Desire.* A qualification common to two of these was that the story itself had a link to jazz. The central figure in *The Man with the Golden Arm* was a jazz-band drummer; and in *I Want to Live* a condemned woman just happened to be a Gerry Mulligan fan.

It was in television, curiously, that what had begun in the motion pictures as a target of opportunity in *The Man with the Golden Arm* and *I Want to Live* became an infectious style, spreading rapidly to every area of underscore writing. Henry Mancini's scoring of a detective serial called *Peter Gunn* was so original, so skillful and so attractive, and its melodies so striking, that record albums of the *Peter Gunn* music sold more than a million copies.

The influence of *Peter Gunn* has been felt more recently in the underscores of a number of familiar TV serials—*The Man from U.N.C.L.E., The Girl from U.N.C.L.E., Secret Agent, T.H.E. Cat, Batman, Ironside, I Spy* and many more—provided by such industrious and ingenious composers as Billy Byers, Robert Drasnin, Gerald Fried, Hugo Friedhofer, Earle Hagen, Quincy Jones, Joe Kirshner, Jack Marshall, Oliver Nelson, Stu Phillips, Pete Rugolo, Lalo Schifrin, Bobby Scott and Richard Shores. The same satisfaction of a requirement for a sophisticated *contemporary* music may be remarked in many TV and radio commercials, including those of Mitch Leigh, the composer of *Man of La Mancha*.

It was Mancini again, and this time in the motion pictures, who broke the link of jazz to crime and lowlife with his scores for *Breakfast at Tiffany's, The Pink Panther* and *Hatari*. Like most of those who have come after him, Mancini is an eclectic writer, more deeply rooted in jazz than in Serious, but easily conversant in both idioms. It might be said of him—and it has been said—that he falls between two stools, that what he writes is neither jazz nor Serious. This is, in a sense, true; but it is also the very circumstance that has given his music its stylistic distinction and its idiomatic importance.

What predestined the motion-picture underscore as the

most promising area of idiomatic reconciliation in music was the fact that it has no tradition or prescribed forms. Each new picture has its own requirements, providing the composer, as he goes from picture to picture, with a variety of challenges posed by the specifications of a variety of dramatic and pictorial situations and the predilections of a wide variety of directors.

The parochial world of jazz, always suspicious of commercial success and jealous of its separate identity, looks down on Mancini; and the equally parochial world of Serious music, with its disdain of any mass medium, is hardly aware of his existence. It is my own belief, however, that between those two stools, right where Mancini is alleged to have fallen, flows the mainstream of contemporary music, accepting contributions from a variety of tributaries ranging from Serious and jazz to rock and electronic. Certainly it is the mainstream of the contemporary lyric theater. The world of Serious music, preoccupied with the troubled present and parlous future of an obsolete European medium known as opera, ignores the fact that the motion picture is the contemporary theater of the twentieth century, just as opera was the contemporary theater of Italy and much of the rest of Europe in the seventeenth, eighteenth and nineteenth centuries.

It is not that the Serious-music community is unaware of the existence of the motion picture, or of its potentiality, although I do not believe that awareness, in this context, is synonymous with understanding. Many Serious composers, as noted earlier, have written film scores. In the infancy of the sound film there was even a lot of operatic activity, both in the United States and abroad, with opera being smuggled into pictures in the form of stories about opera singers, the latter impersonated by the real thing—Lawrence Tibbett, Grace Moore, Richard Tauber, Jan Kiepura, Nino Martini,

Michael Bohnen, Gino Bechi and Miliza Korjus—and such approximations of the real thing as Jeanette MacDonald, Nelson Eddy and Mario Lanza. More recently we have had the filming of opera-house productions—the Salzburg *Der Rosenkavalier,* for example—and in television there have been a number of special opera productions tailored to the requirements and potentiality of the new medium.

But none of all this has worked—quite. Whatever the devices or the technical approach, it represents an effort to superimpose an old form on a new one, or vice versa. And the new form tends to exaggerate rather than disguise the flaws of the old. Opera, because of the set pieces and a pacing prescribed by a score, tends to be more stagebound than the legitimate theater; and the artificiality of dialogue sung rather than spoken, which has plagued opera from the time of its birth in the seventeenth century, becomes insupportable when exposed to the unrelenting eye of the camera and the amplification of the sound track.

Nor do singers look well, as a rule, while singing, not even the handsomest of them; and the camera, inevitably, shortens the distance between singer and spectator that happily modifies the vision in the opera house. Prerecording may remove the most disturbing evidence of effort and distress, but the singer must still pretend to be singing, and the result is only slightly less appalling than the sight of real singing, especially in the close-ups favored by modern directors and photographers.

It is probably idle, therefore, to think of opera in the motion picture in any conventional or traditional sense. An outdated form merely seems more outdated than it does in its native setting. It would be more profitable, I believe, and certainly more realistic, to think of every motion picture as opera in the sense that it represents a combination of theater and music, achieving, as in some of the examples previously cited, something that goes on beyond combination to integration. It is this integration, as illustrated in such a picture as *A Man and a Woman,* that I have in mind when I speak of the motion picture as lyric theater. *A Man and a Woman* won an Oscar in 1966, and Francis Lai's score did not; but most students of the subject would agree that there would have been no Oscar without the score.

The opera lover, I know, will object that there is very little singing in the motion pictures, excepting the motion-picture musicals, and that such singing as occurs from time to time is usually restricted to the "title song." This is true; but there is no reason to assume that the truth is immutable. A singing voice was employed effectively in *A Man and a Woman,* and the example will certainly be acted upon. It is unlikely that we will ever have actors singing in pictures other than the musicals, but that may be all for the best. The singing voice as part of the underscore could well contribute to a more sophisticated kind of musical theater than anything yet achieved by the motion-picture musical, which, as something transplanted from Broadway to the screen, discloses many of the debilities of transplanted opera. Only the music itself is less old-fashioned.

In assessing the potentiality of the motion picture as lyric theater it will be helpful to remind ourselves of certain unsolved problems common to theater and opera alike, and to examine the facilities provided by the motion picture for their solution. All forms of theater, from opera through light opera, operetta, musical comedy and the musical to spoken drama, have always represented less than completely satisfactory adjustments between the contending claims of the lyrical and the prosaic or intellectual. The age-old impulse to elevate the dramatic situation from the prosaic to the lyrical by the introduction of music has been inhibited in the legitimate theater by the impossibility of using music without obscuring the text. An accompanying orchestra gets in the way. The interlude, or incidental music, founders on the problem of what to do on the stage while the music is going on. Both devices have been employed, but the difficulties they create have kept their employment from becoming general. Poetry, rhymed or in blank verse, is the next best lyrical thing; but poetry, if rather less so than song, introduces an element of artifice, or artificiality, hardly compatible with the contemporary taste for natural speech and natural deportment in the theater.

The various forms of specifically musical theater, from opera to the musical, represent a solution weighted in favor of the lyrical. Here the problems inhibiting the legitimate theater's use of music are solved by definition. The accompanying orchestra is surmounted by the singing voice. The nonvocal musical interlude finds accommodation on the stage in the form of ballet or a more choreographic style of acting than is admissible in the legitimate theater. But there is a new problem: how to accommodate the text?

Originally, the narration of the drama was accomplished in opera by dry or accompanied recitative. Full rein was given to the lyrical element at appropriate moments in the form of solo arias and various types of concerted number. But this procedure, in time, was felt to be not entirely satisfactory. The recitative was not musical enough and tended to be dull. The arias and concerted numbers were too musical, and tended to interrupt and detract from the course of narrative and action. In the later stages of opera evolution a compromise was sought in the merging of the prosaic and the lyrical in a kind of continuous parlando, or declamation, delegating ever more lyrical responsibility to the orchestra, a procedure designed to give the listener the best of both worlds. In fact, it gave him a bit of each but denied him the best of either. In the modern operas of our own time we have seen the compromise collapse, with the composers disdaining lyricism even in the orchestra, and achieving a *tour de force* of lunatic nonsense by imposing upon the singers a kind of stilted intonation and stilted prosody less lyrical than speech, while, at the same time, defeating any prosaic objective by setting up such a racket in the orchestra that the words cannot be heard.

In the very earliest form of opera the objective had been to employ music as a handmaiden of the text in a presumably Hellenistic fashion. This ideal was corrupted in the first century of operatic history by public preoccupation with scenic display and, later, by priorities accorded to vocal virtuosity. During the prosperity of *bel canto* in the eighteenth century, both composer and librettist served the singer, with little more expected or desired of the orchestra than the provision of accompaniments and instrumental interludes. A correction in favor of the composer and the orchestra was achieved in the mature operas of Gluck and Mozart; and throughout the nineteenth century the orchestra, as the composer's instrument, grew steadily in importance at the expense of the singer's instrument of the voice.

This can be assessed, in retrospect, as a trend toward the prosaic, determined not so much by the orchestra itself, an essentially lyrical institution, as by the German predilection for ascribing to instrumental music an ideational content, for seeing in the composer a kind of super-philosopher, and for discovering in the orchestra the ultimate instrument of revelation. None of this is necessarily incompatible with the achievement of balance between the lyrical and the prosaic in the theater, as demonstrated by Wagner and in the best

217

operas of Strauss; but subsequent composers have been unable to sustain either the lyrical or the prosaic inspiration of the nineteenth-century German masters. They have been commentators rather than philosophers; saddled, by tradition and convention, with the philosopher's instrument of the symphony orchestra, they have tempted to disguise the poverty of their commentary by the pompous and garrulous employment of the orchestra's many voices.

The evolutionary cycle of opera as a form of lyric theater is, as I have observed, complete, and it has been complete for some time. But we have in the motion picture not only the medium for the introduction of a new cycle, but also a medium in which the technical problems that have previously inhibited the achievement and maintenance of a balance between the lyrical and the prosaic are readily soluble. The motion picture is less dependent than the legitimate theater on continuous conversation, and the propriety of music as a sustaining element, filling silence and accompanying action and movement, is self-evident.

Music can be introduced and withdrawn so inconspicuously that the listener is hardly aware of its arrival, its departure or its effect. Intervals in the action and the text can be filled with music in a way that contributes to the continuity of each. Music can be used descriptively, dramatically and atmospherically. It can heighten tension, build suspense and broaden humor. It can establish and elaborate mood. It can be used for all these things, and it is being so used, more or less, in every motion picture made nowadays anywhere in the world.

Electrical reproduction makes it possible not only to introduce music unobtrusively but also to adjust the balance of music and the spoken word in such a way that the word is not obscured. There has been a certain prejudice on the part of producers and directors against the coincidence of music and dialogue. But coincidence has been tried successfully, and the future is likely to see further experiments in the integration of music and text.

In one respect, however, the evolution of the new lyric theater reverses the sequence of the operatic epoch. Opera began vocally and ended in the orchestra. The lyric theater in the motion pictures began instrumentally, discounting the spoken word, and no one would predict now just what the future role of song, or of the singing voice, will be, discounting song as it is used in the motion-picture musicals.

That there is a place for it has been made persuasively evident in the use of title songs, usually heard as vocal song during the showing of credits at the beginning and end of a picture, and constituting, actually, a kind of overture. Many of these title songs have become formidable moneymakers— Mancini's "Moon River" in *Breakfast at Tiffany's,* for example, or Mandel's "Shadow of Your Smile" in *The Sandpiper.* Such songs as these—and the films have sponsored many more—suggest the possibility of a second golden age of American songwriting, centered this time in Hollywood rather than in New York.

The most stimulating experiment in the use of vocal song thus far has been Michel LeGrand's score for *The Umbrellas of Cherbourg,* in which all the dialogue was sung by offscreen singers, the song synchronized with the movement of the actors' lips. There has been no rush to emulate the modest success of this picture. It may have been ahead of its time. Or it may have seemed old-fashioned in the sense that the procedure was too close to opera.

A more likely approach was that of *A Man and a Woman,* employing an offscreen voice during a situation of silent and troubled intimacy between the principals. Notably successful, too, was the device in *Cat Ballou,* where Jerry Livingston's title song was sung at intervals throughout the picture by Nat King Cole and Stubby Kaye, in costume, as a kind of tongue-in-cheek commentary on the farcical doings of Jane Fonda and Lee Marvin. There was something unself-consciously Hellenistic about that.

Even more promising has been the integration of song and story in pictures employing the rock style, most notably in the Beatles' *A Hard Day's Night* and *Help!,* or, at a higher level of sophistication, in *The Graduate,* where the music of Simon and Garfunkel serves as a kind of counterpoint to the action. Paul Simon has suggested the possibility of pictures originating in the music, and this proposition does not appear to me to be farfetched. Indeed, the Beatles' pictures, and the Monkees' television series, would seem to have done just that. They have, in any case, broken the boundaries implicit in the subordination of music as a background to photography by reversing the roles and the priorities. The picture underscores the music.

The opportunities thus opened to the film composer need not be labored. They are virtually limitless, all deriving from the fact that the motion picture, as a form, is essentially an example of *Gesamtkunstwerk,* if hardly Wagnerian. And every inhibition about the use of the singing voice, of course, evaporates, granting that it is unlikely to be an operatic voice or an operatic type of singing—or, for that matter, an operatic kind of music. Only the inhibition against the presence of the singer standing there singing remains. And that, God knows, is tolerable!

However it develops, the medium is there, the requirements are there, the musical talent is there, and the facilities are there. Music is already so integral an element in motion pictures, and so attractive to the motion-picture public, that most of the major studios have their own music-publishing and recording subsidiaries; and there have been instances where the music for a film has been more profitable than the film itself. Improvements are needed in film recording and in the reproduction facilities of theaters and television sets; but that is a soluble mechanical problem.

Not every picture, certainly, is an example of a high order of lyric theater. But what counts is the fact that many of them *could* be fine lyric theater and some of them *are*. Some pictures lend themselves more readily than others to lyrical elaboration. Some producers and some directors are more sympathetic to music than others. And the change from a European to a modern American musical idiom is still transitional. Nothing dramatic is going to happen between today and tomorrow. But something is happening.

It was inevitable, probably, that the musical talent most hopefully engaged in this phenomenon would come from a new school of composers, free of the constraints and presumptions imposed upon the Serious composer by his nineteenth-century European, and especially German, heritage. The composer working in the motion pictures, unlike his Serious-music counterpart, can accept his profession as craft rather than as a mission. And he can work at it for a living, receiving pay for services rendered in the practice of his vocation. He is, in a sense, rescuing music from its bondage as Art, demonstrating that it can also be useful—and entertaining, even moving.

None of all this has been lost upon the film composers themselves. Hugo Friedhofer, one of the rare individuals among the older generation of film composers who are equally at home with the new generation, has said: "It sometimes occurs to me that we work under very much the same conditions as the old Baroque opera composers. The public in those days didn't want to hear the same things over and over, so the composers had to keep on turning out new works."

Quincy Jones, whose experience as jazz composer-arranger has been augmented by three years of study with Nadia Boulanger, is one of many who see in the motion picture the most promising field of creative composition. "Only in films," he has said, "the good ones, anyway, do you have a chance to express as much as you know musically. The level of music here [Hollywood] is very high, and it's getting better all the time. Everybody is writing the best he can. Where else can you write good music for a living these days? I'm writing closer to what I want than I ever have in my life. As a matter of fact, I believe that the best music being written in this country today is coming out of films."

So do I. And not only in America.

Recapitulation
and Coda

AT THE ROOT of our esthetic troubles, in America and Great Britain, lies Europe; and, in Europe, the nineteenth century. The Europe from which our conventional and fashionable notions of culture derive is no more. The new culture is American, even in Europe; and its art is so offensive to those of traditional European cultural orientation—and they dominate the cultural Establishment everywhere—that it is dismissed as "uncultured," "commercial" and "popular."

The very word "popular," indeed, in the vocabulary of the cultural Establishment throughout the Western democracies, is a contemptuous epithet. And it is this disdain, distrust and even fear of popularity and of popular success that has frustrated, and continues to frustrate, any reasonable or rational assessment of what has happened in music in the twentieth century.

In order to defend itself from the awful truth of Europe's passing, and of the passing of the nineteenth century, the cultural Establishment has conjured up a never-never culture of its own, in which music is withdrawn from everyday life and its withdrawal greeted by self-congratulatory applause as evidence of valiant cultural integrity.

This is true, of course, not only of music. John Canaday, art critic of *The New York Times,* discussing comparable tendencies in the visual arts (June 25, 1961), arrived at conclusions as pertinent to music as to painting and sculpture. Noting the contradiction implicit in the term "museum of modern art," suggesting "a stance with one foot in the grave of the past and the other on the banana peel of the moment," he wrote:

Thus combining impaired vision with precarious footing, critics have come up with some curious expressions leading to further bizarre analyses, thence to even more curious artistic expressions, and so on in a circle of intellectual incest. This circle has been winding like an ingrown hair ever since critic-historians began operating on a double standard by which avant-garde art was found interesting to the extent that it was (a) completely original and (b) the natural consequence of the originality that was immediately contemporary last week.

Instead of following a natural development induced by a truly profound response to life, art can self-consciously set out to do what is anticipated by those who chart it. The fact that the line resembles a roller coaster makes it no less devoid of surprise, and the fact that the swoops and rises and descents may make you catch your breath when you are going along for the ride does not affect the fact that you are in an amusement park, not involved with life itself.

The primary objective of the cultural Establishment—the arts councils, the foundations, the European systems of subsidization, the educational arts curricula, the performing institutions and the critics—appears to be, in my view, the stemming of the tide. In the Establishment's view, of course, the objective is to preserve art from commercial pollution. Its accomplishment has been rather to secure social sanction for a condition of noncompetitiveness, for communicative failure and, indeed, for the renunciation of any communicative responsibility. And immunity from competition and responsibility is as corrupting in the arts as in any other calling.

I am speaking, of course, only of contemporary production. The Establishment discharges its custodial and curatorial obligations well enough. The problem is its assumption of the prerogative of acting as arbiter of what, in the music of our own time, is to be accorded the accolade of art and what is not and its insistence upon a public duty to endorse, sponsor, support and applaud its decisions. Both the assumption and the insistence are, in my opinion, vulnerable.

Neither the American foundations, arts councils and universities nor the European public purse can provide enough hush money to preserve forever the fiction of forward movement, of an emperor alive and fully clothed. Music goes on, and it goes its own way, its characteristics determined by the musical impulses and pleasures of society as a whole, whether those strategically situated like it or don't.

In our own century, and in our own society, the vitality and the production—as demonstrated in ragtime, early jazz, swing, bop, rhythm-and-blues, country-and-western, gospel song, urban blues, folk and pop—have been stupendous, stimulated constantly by new facilities for communication. In no previous culture, probably, has contemporary music been so pervasive a part of the life of so large a percentage of the world's populace.

The Establishment has ignored it all; and a reckoning, I believe, is imminent, if only because so much of what is now being offered as new art music is so patently unmusical

225

that even some of the Establishment are beginning to murmur. As long as what they were given could be related to music, even if only theoretically, they could grit their teeth, play the game and keep their misgivings to themselves.

But the latest accomplishments of pan-Webern serialism and the electronics laboratories, against which Webern sounds like Puccini, are too much. This may be acoustics. It may even have potentiality as a musical auxiliary. It may be capable of being put to musical use. But it is not music. And a great many sober individuals in the Establishment know it. I take it as rather more than merely a straw in the wind when Sir Jack Westrup, in an editorial in *Music and Letters* (January 1968), observes:

> The whole practice of "please-yourself" music has now reached a stage when any kind of idiocy asks to be taken seriously. A piano is not simply an instrument to be played. It is a piece of furniture which allows you to crawl underneath it and beat tattoos on its underside. Some time ago a critic remarked with apparent approval: "A slapped trombone is a glorious sound." These are strong words; but if "glorious" is to be accepted, they could be applied equally well to a coal scuttle. . . .
>
> The critics might help if they were to refuse to take this sort of thing seriously; but too often they seem to be afraid of the possible reproach that they are old-fashioned, or else they are so weary of the drug of familiar music that anything new is welcome. If to be sane is to be old-fashioned, it is a pity that there are not more old-fashioned musicians about. . . . Experiment is the lifeblood of music; but those who experiment might well ask themselves whether there is not something to be said for communicating to others. A momentary triumph of complete absurdity before an audience of twenty-five people may, for the time being, satisfy composers who walk blinkered through the world. But this is not the reward that serious artists seek.

A few months after the appearance of this cogent advice, the London critics blandly illustrated Sir Jack's point. They dutifully attended an offering by the Focus Opera Group entitled "Three? Avant-Garde? Operas?" And they dutifully recounted their experience in the following Sunday's papers (March 17). According to Desmond Shawe-Taylor, music critic of the *Sunday Times,* who devoted 1,200 words to the subject under a four-column heading: HOW MANY PING-PONG BALLS MAKE AN OPERA? this is what they sat through:

Electronic rumbles and thumps became audible; a man draped silver foil and coloured streams round a music-stand (it fell down later, but what of that?) and aimed Ping-Pong balls at a waste-paper basket (with scant success, but what of that?) ; two clowns interminably shot more Ping-Pong balls at one another (dropping them nearly all, but what of that?) ; another man tinkered (or pretended to tinker?) with guitar, xylophone and flex; he might have caused some of the electronic noises, or not. The first man took off his shoes and socks and put on sandals; he blew up a balloon, and rubbed it horribly with Stockhausen-like amplification. . . .

Some of Shawe-Taylor's colleagues doubtless felt that his bemusement was ill placed. Michael Parsons, writing for the *Musical Times* (May 1968) , found that in this composition (Cornelius Cardew's *Schooltime Compositions*) :

sound and action, instead of underlining each other, simply co-existed; interaction arose from the coincidence, overlapping and juxtaposition in space and time of simultaneous activities—something Cardew would consider more interesting than relationships contrived according to a set plan. Quiet, long-held vocal and instrumental sounds, sometimes electronically amplified and distorted, merged or drew apart in ways which drew one's attention to every slight alteration. John Pitchford gave a performance with newspaper, balloons and other assorted objects which was most inventive when purely and unselfconsciously meaningless, while Robin Page and Eric Brown played a clownish ball game which leant more towards entertainment, demonstrating that any activity can be interesting to watch for its own sake, particularly when taken out of its usual context.

Lest it be inferred that this kind of hopeful credulity, suggesting the gaping yokel at a medicine show, is confined to British criticism, I hasten to include the following from Theodore Strongin's account (in *The New York Times* of August 9, 1968) of Stanley Silverman's "occult opera" *Elephant Steps* as performed at Tanglewood under the auspices of the Berkshire Music Center and thanks to the generosity of the Fromm Foundation:

Does it have a plot? Well, there's this character, Reinheart . . . or are there two Reinhearts? And who is Hartman? Reinheart is in bed as the "opera" begins. He falls out of bed several times. There's a doctor in the room. A man (Hartman?) comes in the room. He goes out and is trapped in a wall with his head showing in the room. He has two large shaggy white hands. Everyone is preoccupied with hands. Then there's a radio station. Does Hartman get on the air or doesn't he? It's not clear. And so on until the end when Reinheart (or was it Hartman?) climbs up a ladder and stays there.

Strongin, like Parsons, found this sort of thing pretty significant. The composer and the librettist, he said, "are courageous men. What they have done is taken all the senses, not just hearing, and given them equal value. They have stretched the awareness. Reinheart's falling out of bed, for instance, has the same function as a musical note or accent. So does a green light bulb that keeps going on and off, irregularly but often, and a silent film loop in which a man takes gloves out of his pocket and puts them on over and over again. In a stream of consciousness way, *Elephant Steps* has form."

Not that there hasn't been worse. Peter Yates, in his *Twentieth Century Music* (1967), tells us how LaMonte Young "stuffed a violin with concert programs and burned it in public performance" and how David Tudor "attacked a piano with chisel, rubber hammer and bicycle chain and, on another occasion, with a saw." Yates also cites, approvingly, an exercise carried out at the San Francisco Tape Music Center: "The four glass sides of a tropical fish tank are painted with a musical staff and with squares indicating *arco, pizzicato,* etc. Four instrumentalists sit one at each side. Six fish, white or black, placed in the water, swim behind staves and boxes to furnish notes and instructions. Several weeks of practising were needed to enable the players to keep up with the fish."

Music critics do not, as a rule, praise these obscenities, but neither, as a rule do they protest, by word or example, that the specatacle of adult musicians tossing Ping-Pong balls, or falling into and out of bed, or taking musical dictation from fish is beneath the dignity of a Serious critic. They attend, they remain and they devote valuable newspaper and magazine space to an account of what they have seen and heard. The great majority of them, as Sir Jack suggests, are running scared—or behaving like ostriches.

They gambled, from despair rather than courage or conviction, on serialism, and the rest of the Establishment with them. Now that this anti-musical procedure is ending, inexorably, in the computer, they are the victims of their own timidity, and they are the victims, more significantly, of their own cultural bias.

A Peter Heyworth, for example, in the *High Fidelity* article previously cited, can say: "Like other mortals, a critic has no choice but to accept the period he lives in even if he doesn't like it." But Heyworth is speaking here not of jazz, or rock, or pop, none of which is mentioned in the 3,000 words of his text, but of—Stockhausen! For Peter Heyworth, and for most of his Serious-music-critic colleagues everywhere, the music of several hundreds of millions of people in every part of the globe is irrelevant to a discussion of music in the 1960s.

So far is he from accepting the period in which he lives that he resigns himself, with the docility characteristic of today's Serious-music-critic fraternity, to something in which, according to Stockhausen himself, any distinction between music and mere sound has finally disappeared. Also missing, one is tempted to add, is any connection between music and people.

What is one to make, for example, of the *Computer Cantata* by Lejaren Hiller, director of the Experimental Music Studio at the University of Illinois, which, according to an accompanying booklet of twenty-two double-spaced typewritten pages, "presents the result of a series of studies in computer composition carried out in the spring of 1963 . . . to test the efficiency and ease of MUSICOMP (MUsic SImulator-Interpreter for COMpositional Procedures), a completely generalized programming scheme for musical composition intended for use with an IBM 7090 computer. . . . It also includes two studies of computer synthesis carried out with a second computer, the CX–1 . . . that permits compositional results to be converted directly into computer generated sound"?

When Hiller's colleague at Illinois, Herbert Brün, "performed" his *Non Sequitur* (1966) at the London Institute of Contemporary Arts exhibition, "Cybernetic Serendipity," in August 1968, an interviewer from the *Daily Telegraph* observed that tune and the heart must come in somewhere. "What's the heart got to do with it?" Brün wanted to know. "Some emotions, sure, but the heart—just a metaphor, ridiculous scientifically."

The critics, to return to Sir Jack, are also running lazy. They simply will not get off their beat to find out what has been going on in music for the past half century. If it doesn't happen in the concert hall, the opera house or the church it is not music as far as they are concerned. Nor will they address themselves to anything but Serious music even when it can be heard on their own home ground in the concert hall, as is often the case nowadays. They leave it to the jazz critics or the pop critics or, as in the case of the musical, to the dramatic critics, arguing that these others are better qualified to judge. That the argument is unexceptionable hardly speaks well for those who call themselves music critics, nor is it any excuse for ignorance.

The consequences of this auto-segregation, this "opting out" from society both by composers and by critics, will be with us for a long time, particularly in the United States, which, with its hundreds of university schools of music and the largesse of the gullible foundations, has provided nearly impregnable warrens for those who believe that computation and electricity, not the human heart and spirit, make music. But something is happening, and it is happening, as usual, in the least likely of places—in pop.

It would seem now, in retrospect, that there never was a chance that any considerable number of the Serious-music community could be persuaded of the artistic virtue of jazz and the jazz musician. New Orleans and Dixieland were felt to be too primitive; swing was too closely identified with dancing and bop, curiously, was too esoteric, while the new, or free, jazz has been too close to Serious music's own obstreperous and eccentric avant-garde. In the view of the Serious-music community, I suspect, one avant-garde was enough. They couldn't disavow their own; but there was no need to compound the mischief and the din by welcoming another.

But not a few in the Serious-music community have found pop palatable who could never stomach jazz; and neither the sometimes excellent quality of the lyrics nor the reversion to pre-Baroque melodic and harmonic practices can explain quite adequately why. Indeed, one would have assumed a preference for jazz, if only because of the harmonic sophistication of its mature forms and the superior virtuosity of its best musicians.

It is possible, of course, that some Serious musicians and Serious critics have sensed in later jazz styles, and especially in hard bop and the New Jazz, familiar symptoms of decadence. But few of them will have heard enough of either to arrive at such critical conclusions. A more likely explanation, for the Serious-music community as a whole, is that in pop, as opposed to jazz, the exotic African element, while actually stronger, has been less obvious.

Most of the Serious-music community know little or nothing of the origins of pop in rhythm-and-blues, gospel song and country-and-western, or of the extent of the African influence in contemporary country-and-western. Nor have they followed the evolution of the blues from country blues through rhythm-and-blues to the urban blues of the present. Thus, when they are exposed to the new post-jazz black music through the intermediary of the white pop groups, especially such English groups as the Beatles, the Rolling Stones and the Cream, they react innocently, so to speak, accepting the dilution without concerning themselves with the sources. Pop is not only more varied in its sources than jazz was forty years ago, but also more varied in its manifestations. The visitor from the outside has more to choose from.

It may also be true that in the present Afro-American epoch, the relationship between white and black may be entering a new phase in the evolution of Western music. The young white musician, less shackled by diatonic harmonic tradition than the young white musician of the early jazz and swing eras, is free to offer more of his own native musicality without total stylistic dependence upon Afro-American example.

Pop, at the same time, is being enriched, particularly on records, by the imaginative and sophisticated guidance of a new type of creative musician, an unadvertised *deus ex machina* in the form of a musical director, most familiarly represented by the Beatles' George Martin. It is also being enriched by the participation in the studios of older professional musicians, frequently jazz musicians.

It seems inevitable that jazz musicians will be drawn more and more into pop, if only because the two styles need each other. Pop has thus far been predominantly a vocal style, despite all the noise of electric guitars and organs—which is all to the good—and jazz, having divorced itself from the Popular singer at the close of the swing era, has been too exclusively instrumental. Pop needs the jazz musician's instrumental skills and experience if it is to grow, while jazz needs the vocal and melodic innocence of pop.

There is no fundamental idiomatic incompatibility. Both are products of the Afro-European fusion that has determined the musical course of the century. The jazz musician will find his way back to the mainstream or perish in the more or less benign lunacy of the avant-garde; and the pop musician can use him in achieving musical maturity.

The older Serious musician is not about to switch to pop or jazz, although some Serious critics, as noted earlier, have begun to take pop seriously—too seriously, probably, for pop's own good. Nor could he, in most cases, overcome the idiomatic incompatibility. But his juniors are already growing up with pop, and some are excelling in it; and the older musician's reaction is often less negative than it would have been a generation or so ago had his children taken to jazz.

Many younger musicians, however, who forty or fifty years ago would have chosen a career exclusively in Serious music are being drawn to a more truly contemporary idiom—as performers, composers, arrangers, counselors, technicians, producers, etc.—and are not overlooking the challenging and promising medium of the motion-picture underscore. The Establishment, and especially the educational Establishment, will have to follow suit. It is, indeed, already doing so, as is demonstrated by the institution of courses in *useful* composition and arranging in some of the university conservatories.

The Establishment's most formidable bastion remains society's acceptance of a concept of art as a kind of mystery—above and beyond the pleasures of the senses, separate and distinct from, and superior to, entertainment, amusement and diversion; of the artist as a source of revelation, a high priest answerable only to his assumed genius, and of art patronage as a secular and intellectual counterpart of church attendance as evidence of culturally enlightened good citizenship.

An extension of this curious notion—curious because so much of what we now celebrate as ultimate artistic accomplishment in the masterpieces of earlier times originated as entertainment and diversion—is the notion that art must be serious, sober, solemn and *meaningful;* that *enjoyment,* which may involve a high level of discrimination, is somehow "mindless," as if discrimination were not a mental or intellectual accomplishment; that any artistic enterprise solemnly and seriously intended is, therefore, worth taking seriously and that seriousness itself is somehow intrinsically virtuous and the pursuit of pleasure intrinsically sinful.

In music, to be culturally *in* is to think of music as something to be *understood* and to be thought of as belonging to an elite capable of *understanding*. The appreciation of Serious music is applauded as a *cerebral* achievement; the enjoyment of Popular music is disdained as *visceral* and assumed to be undiscriminating. And in order to make *understanding* appear admirable and exceptional, new music is valued as art in proportion to the show it makes of being difficult to get at, resistant to comprehension and assimilation—obscure, complex and even absurd.

In this schedule of values no credit at all is applied to any new music's capacity to give pleasure. Rather the contrary. New music comes off best that purposefully and methodically gives pain—or bores the listener out of his wits. The attitude of the Establishment toward the delights of the senses would make a Quaker meeting look like a Witches' Sabbath.

By one of those feats of intellectual prestidigitation in which the Establishment displays an astonishing virtuosity, Art has been divorced from art; and any rational and reasonable artistic accomplishment, as far as contemporary production is concerned, can lead to anathema and excommunication. The kind of professional who, in healthier times, would have been regarded as the ultimate artist may now be disparaged as "commercial," while the poseur who formerly would have been dismissed as a dilettante or eccentric now passes for an Artist and is protected from unfavorable comparison with the true professional by categorical discrimination.

The Establishment sees it differently, of course. Peter Yates offers a probably typical rationalization when he says: "The term *creation*, the idea of "creating" a work of art, are modern, signifying the individualism and isolation which have become, in our minds, inseparable from the artistic effort. Craftsmanship, the excellent performance of a skilled job, is *by the same amount* [italics added] lessened."

The principal difficulty, therefore, in reassessing our own artistic condition lies in ridding ourselves of the concept of art as a profession or calling and of culture as a social ornament. Art is no more a profession than excellence is a profession, or mediocrity. It is a distinction, the name we give to a superior craft of communication—music, painting, theater, literature, etc.; and the artist is, or should be, the master craftsman. Nor is culture a sterile ornament. A society's culture is its own conduct, its own production, its own enthusiasms and its own discrimination, not its ritual adoration of Bach and Beethoven or its joyless awe of Stockhausen and Pierre Boulez.

That is the way many of today's excellent "commercial" craftsmen view their profession; and their accomplishments may, in time, be appreciated as art. Much of what passes as Art in contemporary Serious music cannot forever escape exposure as a desperate and patently outrageous sham; and it is not, therefore, utopian to anticipate the eventual dispelling of such stifling superstitions as the incompatibility of art and commerce, the indecency of the artist as entertainer and the immunity of art from the discipline of supply and demand.

"Over and over again," wrote John Russell Taylor, film critic of the London *Times*, in his discussion of a festival of films of the 1920s at the National Film Theater (July 28, 1968), "the old rule has been proving itself, that in the cinema nothing is more generally destructive to the production of art than the conscious aim of doing exactly that. How often does it not prove that the films of forty years back which made a great parade of their artistic aspirations now look desperately faded, artificial, pretentious, while those which were made with no other explicit aim than to divert still hold up and look, indeed, probably better than ever."

The old rule is as applicable to music as to motion pictures. How much of what we most admire in the standard repertoire of Serious music was not also made "with no other explicit aim than to divert?" What counts, from an esthetic point of view, is that there are many kinds and levels of diversion and entertainment. What counts, from the professional's point of view, is that no diversion is possible without the prior establishment of communication; and communication cannot be established without regard for an audience's own language, habits and predilections. These prescribe the professional's frame of reference, and for the true artist the implied discipline need not be unwelcome.

For only his communicative success with his public as an articulate, intelligible and *fascinating* member of society can assure him the satisfaction of his calling. The public is a capricious and fallible arbiter; but it is the least fallible of any and, in the long run, the only one that matters. Most fallible of all is the artist himself. And society's concession to the artist, toward the end of the nineteenth century, of the prerogative of judging his own work and the work of his peers, and its abdication to the artist of responsibility for determining idiom and style, signaled the end of the very cultural prosperity which concession and abdication were meant to ensure.

Given this freedom to do as they pleased, artists have behaved like adolescents who, released from parental restraint, first seek the limits of what is still permissible. When they discover that there are no limits, that anything goes, the taste

237

of freedom sours. The parent becomes an object of contempt, and the boy—or girl—turns insolent. The end is reached when even insolence is applauded. "I threw the urinal in their faces as a challenge," said Marcel Duchamp, one of the original Dadaists, "and now they admire it for its esthetic beauty."

What Addison wrote in the *Spectator* on April 3, 1711, about art's having to conform to taste would have been laughed down in 1911. But the cultural history of the past fifty years should restrain the laughter today. "Music, architecture and painting, as well as poetry and oratory," he said, "are to deduce their laws and rules from the general sense and taste of mankind, and not from the principles of those arts themselves."

Ignorance, defiance and neglect of this simple and reasonable stricture precipitated the decline and hastened the decay of European culture; and in the twentieth century they have inhibited not only a just appreciation of our own culture but even a common recognition or acknowledgment of what our culture is. What Addison wrote was true then, and it is true now. The quality of a society's arts depends not upon its artists but upon what it demands from its artists. A permissive society will get what it permits. And it will deserve what it gets.

Our own society, as distinct from its cultural Establishment, has done well, and especially in music. Offered a reputable contemporary music that it could not stomach, it has produced an often excellent disreputable music of its own, establishing an idiomatic revolution comparable in its evolutionary implications to the idiomatic revolutions that took place in Europe in the fourteenth and seventeenth centuries.

But gulled by the pervasive mystique of *serious* as opposed to *entertaining,* and of *art* as opposed to *commerce,* this same society continues to heed the value judgments and nourish the vanity of a cultural Establishment which knows little of all this and despises what it knows; a somnolent Establishment, obese and obsolescent, but still greedy, which has spawned and continues to sponsor, in its contemporary production, a degradation and debasement of the arts, a mortification of the senses, a mockery of intelligence, a repudiation of the spirit and a celebration of impotence, impudence and incompetence unexampled in the annals of mankind.

Index

Butler, Joe, 197
Butterfield, Paul, 195
Buxtehude, Dietrich, 88
Byas, Don, 92
Byers, Billy, 212
Byrd, Charlie, 139

Caffarelli (Gaetano Majorano), 88
Cage, John, 17, 25, 77, 200
California, University of (Berkeley), 57
Callas, Maria, 87–88, 130
Calloway, Cab, 54
Canaday, John, 224
Cardew, Cornelius, 227
Caribbean Islands, 51
Carson, Fiddling John, 174, 175
Carter, Benny, 134
Carter Family, 174, 180
Caruso, Enrico, 26, 31
Cash, Johnny, 174
castrato, 145
Catalani, Angelica, 105
Cat Ballou (film), 220
Chailley, Jacques, 116
Charles, Ray, 121, 156, 186
Charles, Teddy, 157
Chase, Gilbert, 116–17
Chávez, Carlos, 17
Checker, Chubby, 172
"Cherokee" (Ray Noble), 142, 143
Cherry, Don, 160
Cherubini, Luigi, 87, 100
Chicago, 55, 176, 178, 186, 194
Chopin, Frédéric, 75, 81, 85
Chorley, Henry F., 112
Christian, Charlie, 130, 177
Christy, June, 164, 168
Clair, René, 204
Clark, Petula, 195

Clarke, Kenny, 136
Classic epoch, 90, 100, 101, 106
Clayton, Buck, 92
Clementi, Muzio, 75
Cliburn, Van, 130
Clooney, Rosemary, 164, 168
Colbran, Isabella, 87
Cole, Nat King, 23, 130, 164, 166, 179, 186, 220
Coleman, Bill, 92
Coleman, Ornette, 60, 129, 149, 151, 153, 160, 200
Collier, Graham, 129–30
Coltrane, John, 130, 136, 147, 153, 158
Columbo, Russ, 19
Como, Perry, 23, 164, 168
composer-arrangers, 125, 128, 129, 133–35, 157, 169, 170, 200, 207–11
composers, 32, 47–48, 91, 102, 104–6, 109–11, 115–17, 119, 228–29, 231
  and films, TV, etc., 50, 202–14, 218, 220–22, 234
  and jazz, 55–56, 92, 156, 157, 200, 201
  and opera, 217–18, 228–29
  and performers, 75–78, 85–89
  and style, 81–89
  and university positions, 122–23
computer, 229–31
concerto grosso, 34, 72, 108
Condon, Eddie, 186, 195
Connor, Chris, 164, 168
Conover, Willis, 22, 96–97
Consul, The (Menotti), 199
Contemporary Music Project of Creativity in Music Education, 129
cool jazz, 52, 59, 139, 142, 163
Copans, Sim, 22